I0530723

# WHISTLEBLOWER

## Exposing Shopify's E-Commerce Scandal

C. ELLISON

Ordering Information:

Prime Seven Media
518 Landmann St.
Tomah City, WI 54660

Printed in the United States of America

# TABLE OF CONTENTS

When I thought of opening the store's I went to Google to research what products would be ideal for an online store. Also, I considered the prices of the items, because I wanted to make it affordable to customers. I was thinking Shopify has a variety of apps that can be used to enhance the products and assist in converting sales. It seems so good to be true, yet my nightmare was just beginning. I wrote this to bring awareness to individuals who have Ecommerce stores at Shopify of my horrifying experiences. I believe that even though other people may have experiences and others who had questionable experiences yet do not know what to do. I contemplated if this was even the right choice to expose them for what I went through or should I just cut my losses and just walk away. However, people are spending their hard-earned money being victimized without even knowing it. I must warn you that what I am about to show you can be very disturbing, but it will help you to understand if you're encountering similar situations or to be aware to know if something is potentially wrong.

I am an ecommerce business owner that had previous stores in the past. I had experiences that were unexplainable, and I did not have the evidence to prove that a company used abuse of power. My previous stores individuals would come to me and express how they loved the items from my store. However, I would look at the sales and not see the purchases. I would reach out to Shopify support only to be informed that the individuals were not being honest. Unfortunately, those stores closed and later I decided to give it another chance. I opened a men's fashion store in which was notated eye-catching and social media was loving my posts and complimenting the items. I sold an item and Shopify stated I needed to pay for the item for the customer paying me. However, they never transferred the money to me and stated I needed to pay them. Mind blogging, how did I owe them in which left me clueless? I paid the monthly fees, paid and organic traffic for over 4 months and I knew something was unethical, but I could not prove it. I received a call that my brother was ill and then found out the same week that he had less than 6 months to live with a chronic illness. My attention was no longer on the store I was back and forth visiting him, yet he died around 3 months.

I needed time to heal from the dark place I was in (traumatic event) and so I relocated out of state. I begin to work and begin to meet new people. I tried to get back the person that I knew, but that person was no longer the same. During that time, I fought depression, anxiety, and met a friend who helped me to heal. So, I decided that opening a new store would be a good way to start. The store opened in July 2023 named Kool Shades 1in which is a sunglass and phone case store. The store website is http://koolshade1.com and is always having updates with new arrivals. I was proud that I designed it and was complimented on social media on how nice the store features are as well as the affordable low prices (of some of the items). I immediately started with paid advertising and organic advertising for over 7 different sources. I went as far as to have a black Friday with 50% off sales. My prices on the products ranged from $11-$200. I placed the top conversions on the website as the following: Mail Champ, Gro One Click Upsell, Pasilous Turbo Speed, Booster Page Speed Optimizer, Thrive By Shop Inventory, Rep AI Concierce, Trust Reviews, Twik, Egg Flow Instant Upsell, Eggflow Instant Traffic, Monster Cart Upsell+Free Gifts, Unlimited AI Smart Upsell Offers, Elfsight Social Share Button, and Smartli AI SED Optimizer Blog.

I decided to gain more exposure decided to make a Google Business page for my store. Consequently, I was in shock that Kool Shades 1 was already on Google with a symbol different from my store. I reached out to Google support to inform them that I did not make this page and I did not know what was going on. I informed them, like all other businesses I like to add products and design them the way I like to and receive a code for confirmation to verify my identity. Google support asked if I could hold for a few minutes and came back like in shock asking me how I wanted to move forward. The site stayed up for nearly a month before it was removed, and my site was placed on Google. So, Google Analysis 4 (GA4) was crossing over to GA4 and so I made sure I was compliant. Instead, I was feeling like it was one battle after another with adding the GA4 onto the store and it was not showing after, yet it was active before. So, my store was not showing the graphics for conversions through Google.

I constantly stayed in contact with Shopify in which they made me feel like I was crazy, or it is not what I am seeing. There was always an explanation or let's see how we can resolve this. I then switched to Go Daddy as my server and the experience was a nightmare. Go Daddy had made a server as well as an account for payment. I contacted them regarding this, and they were in shock when I changed the DNS that they changed it back. This repeatedly happened until I threatened, I would sue them. I was using security for my website named Sucuri and when I found out it was connected to Go Daddy, I did not renew it. As a result, I transferred back to Shopify. I increased traffic from various paid sources, social media (Facebook ads), and search engine paid sources. I was in constant contact with Shopify support regarding the store, because it was too much traffic and signs to know if something was wrong.

Moving forward, I received an email from an Ecom store stating they were building Ecom stores on Facebook (Ecom websites LLC-CEO Amer) at $20 a store design. I was like wow that sounds like a great deal. I immediately ordered a store that was designed professionally, webinars, and at an affordable rate. I named the store Pet Pazzazz after researching a good niche for profit on Google.com. I promoted traffic from this store immediately and was confident that it would catch the eye with discounts and pet lovers. Pet Pazzazz offers accessories as the following: bedding, food, clothes, and toys. Pet Pazzazz can be located at https://petpazzazz.store. The store was open in June, and I was experiencing issues with the store, so I contacted support. I was reassured that everything was fine, and I need to give it some time. I started to research online to search for anything that can help me to understand what was going on with issues constantly happening. I left the stores alone for some days, because I was so stressed and did not know what to do. However, I did receive login information from Ecom store

Address: https://admin.shopify.com/store/91bbfe-2
Login Email: ch77ellison123@hotmail.com
Password: CharleneEllison8277

I changed my email address and password for just a sense of security. However, there was a twist to that if I was logged into the store and someone used the address (https://admin.shopify.com/store/91bbfe-2) they can enter as well. I came back to the store looking into every area and I found a duplicate Pet Pazzazz store that was active and functioning under https://petpazzazz.store/?ab=0&_fd=0&_sc=1. I want you to look at the design of my store.

My Original Store

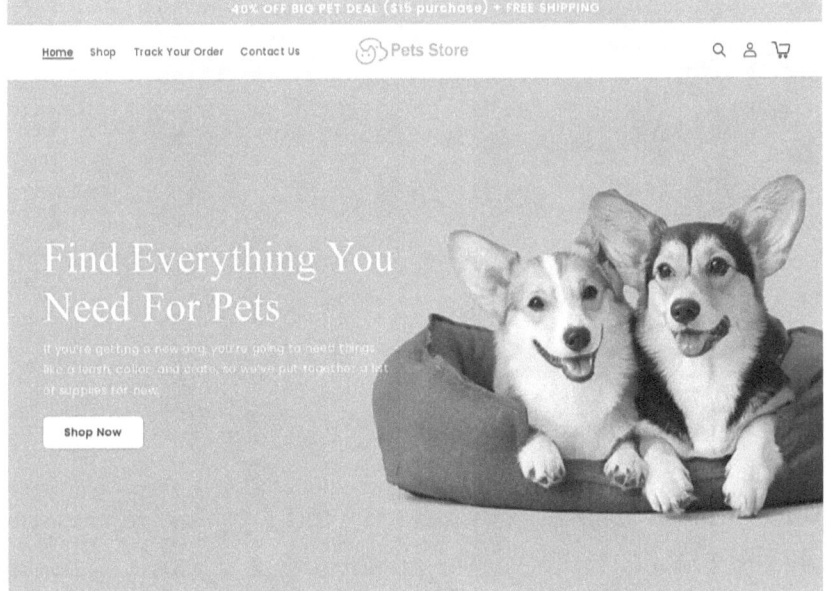

This is the design that was made under Shopify themes under Dawn, had DO NOT REMOVE! It was different from Kool Shade did not state DO NOT REMOVE, but it was something I am about to show that is quite disturbing.

You can imagine how I felt when I saw this. I conducted research to both links to DiiB Answer Engins and it is active (It has a site map, SSL certificate, and recommendations. In contrast,

Kool Shades 1 asked me to publish it yet in reality the free stores are linked to your link already. site it is asking me to publish it. WOW!!!

Diib Answer Engine

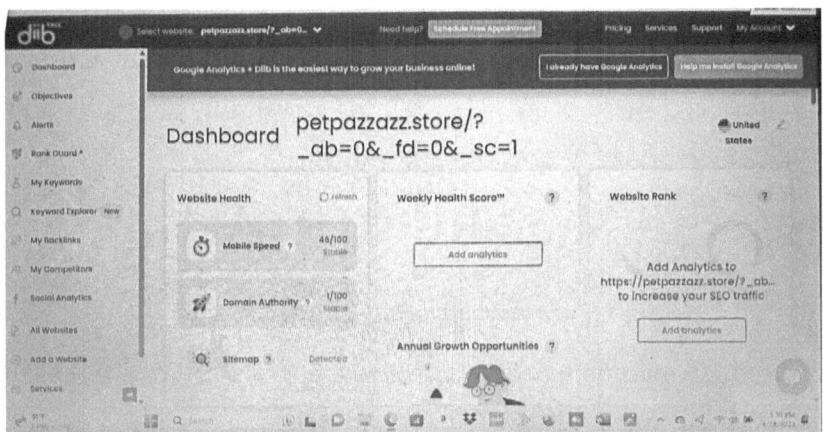

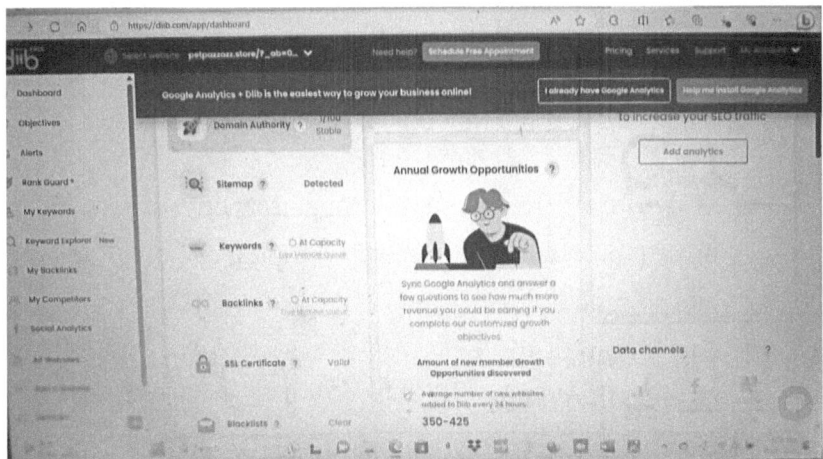

As a result, I decided to place another drop shipping Trendsi to the store to see how it would increase sells. I selected sunglasses that allow customers to see how the glasses would be with individuals wearing them. The traffic was going to the stores, and I was running a test. Almost a week went by, I wanted to look at Trendsi to see how it was going. My store with them had been changed to show their line and I was not able to sign in. It was very confusing, and I reached out to them to explain what had happened that I was not able to sign in. How can we fix this issue? I received an email stating send a picture or screenshot. I wanted to stay positive, but this cycle was becoming draining physically, mentally, and emotionally. I sent another email to them.

Trendsi
Hi Charlene,

Welcome! You probably have some questions about Trendsi. Don't worry, other users did too. That's why we have put together this **Help Center** to help you get started and we have included all the FAQ's that we get most often as well.

We also recommend the following if you haven't done so already:

- **Download** Trendsi mobile app: set up account info, browse products and purchase samples, import products, and so much more!
- **Apple App Store**
- **Google Play Store**
- **Can't find answers?** Reply to this email or access the live chat button in the lower right corner of the Help Center and our 24/7 Customer Support team is there to help!

In the next couple of days, we will be sending you more information and guidance on how to use our platform.

Best,
**The Trendsi Team**

Then I received this information from Trendsi,

| **Dear Charlene:** |
| --- |
| As of June 28, 2023, 12:51 AM, a total of <u>1 Trendsi Products</u> have been successfully added to your Shopify Store: Kool Shades 1 LLC. |
| Best,<br>Trendsi Support |

What I cannot understand is there where multiple traffic utilized since June and now my accounts have a glitch and cannot show the sells or my account above when it was registered.

Unfortunately, I reached out to the supplier Spocket who is the supplier for Shopify. I had noticed the order had been removed from my site they have, and I reached out to them over 4 days, and they would not replace it. I asked them if I had an order how would I know? They asked me to screenshot or take a picture yet on their end they can clearly see what is wrong. I began to have thoughts or questions and I asked Shopify support who takes the payment for the stores. The Shopify support stated Shopify and / or the supplier Spocket. The Shopify support also stated that she has a store as well and when I spoke with another support about an activity on my store she disconnected, because of what I asked (as if she was caught off guard).

# Kool Shade 1- Spocket account (Supplier)

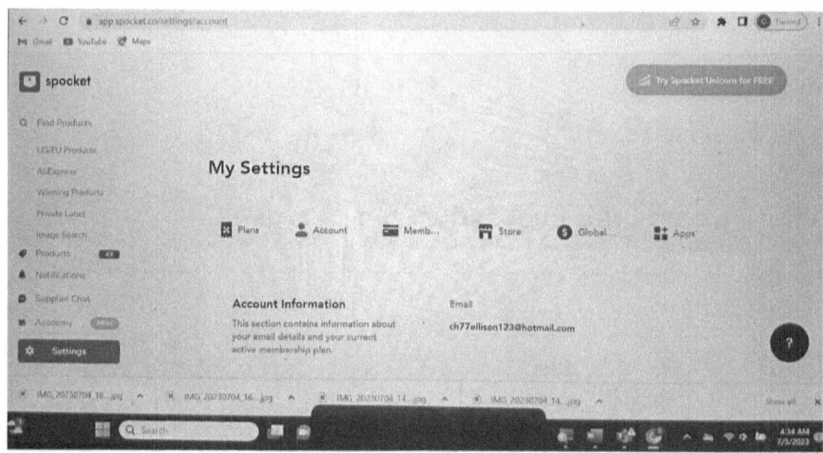

# Pet PetPazzazz- Spocket Supplier

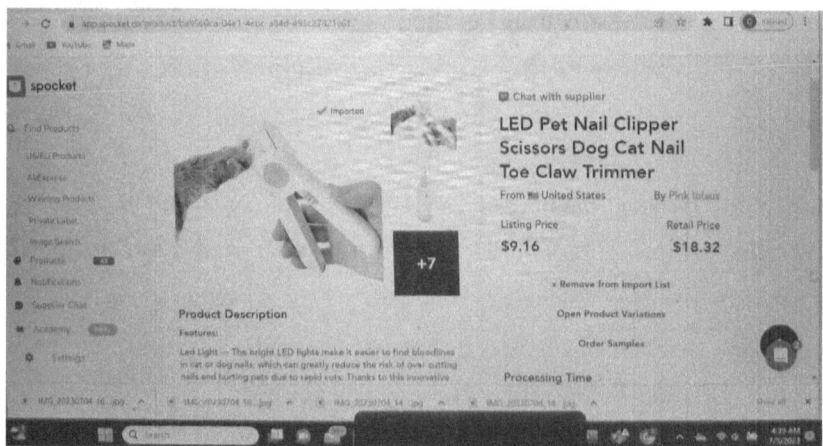

# Spocket Order Track Steps

1. Head over to your **Orders Tab** on the Spocket app
2. Scroll down to the order you are inquiring about
3. Select the truck icon to obtain more details on the shipping status

4. To check the processing and shipping time of the order, click on the product's image

This my email to Spocket

Re: My store is Pet Pazzazz and my orders tab has been removed from my ...

Inbox
Search for all messages with label Inbox
Remove label Inbox from this conversation

| | Jul 11, 2023, 12:26 PM |
| --- | --- |
| **Edrielle from Spocket** | |
| <edrielle@spocket.co> | |

to me

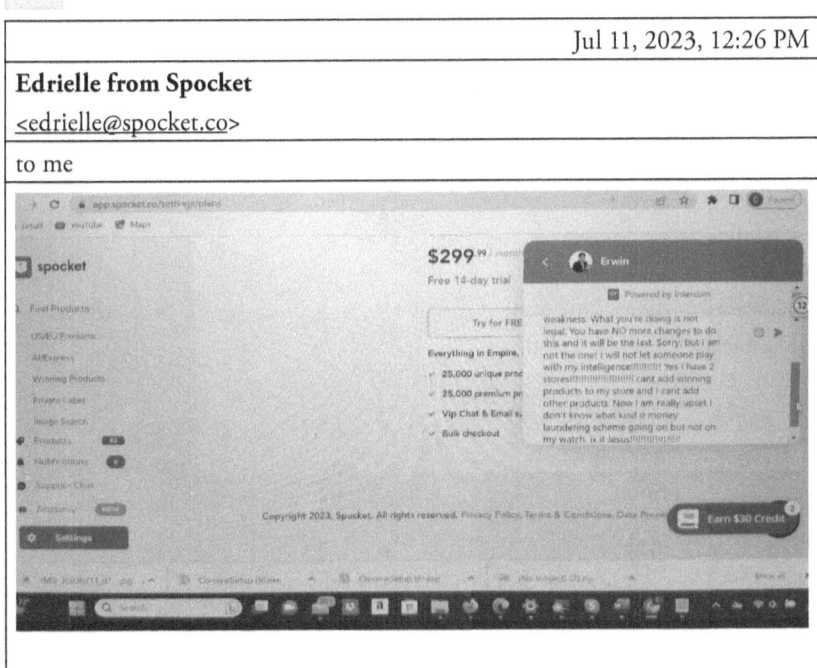

The above picture exhibits a conversation I had with support informing the I know they know the tab is missing and it does not just disappear.

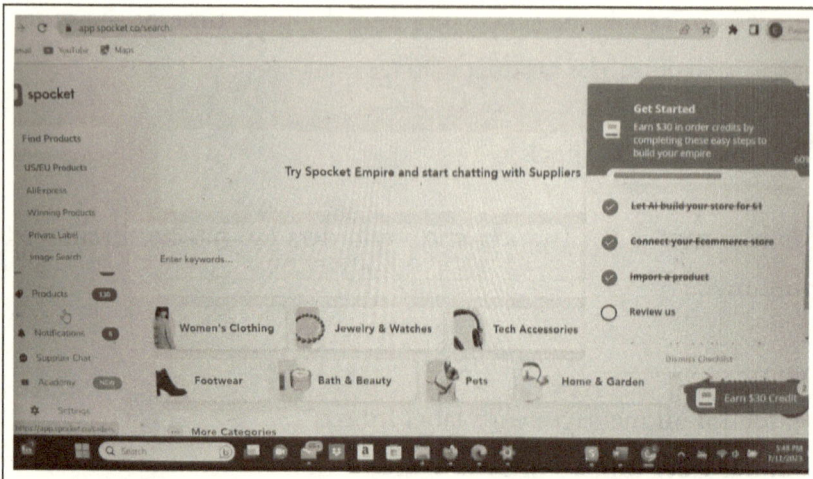

The above picture when you look to the lower left panel there is a space now that looks like it has been whitened out, when I click on it the orders tab will appear. This continued to occur throughout the store's duration. They continuously reached out to me for a review on the right side and emails, yet I never gave them one.

Hi Charlene!

Thanks for reaching out to us. Edrielle stepping in on behalf of Erwin while he's away.

My sincere apologies for any inconvenience. This is never the experience we want you to have, and we appreciate the feedback and we're currently looking for the best way to assist you. Please let me get back to you once I have an update or if we need more information to proceed.

Meanwhile, please feel free to message me should you have other questions or concerns.

Regards,
Edrielle
Customer Support Specialist

| |
|---|
| **Edrielle** |
| Spocket |
| |
| Powered by **Intercom** |
| |
| On Tue, Jul 11, 2023, at 12:13 PM, "Charlene Ellison" <predoc25@gmail.com> wrote: |
| |
| My store is Pet Pazzazz and my orders tab has been removed from my store. I have asked before to place it back. I don't know why it would be moved. I have emailed three times. I'm being calm.....this continues then it's not a mistake it's like harassment or discrimination. I can't put winning items in my store or even add more products unblock my account. |

When I went back to check my emails, I noticed Shopify had sent me an email stating that a sister partner of Shopify wanted to know my preference to give them my personal information. When I opened the store, I checked that I did not want my information given out or sold to anyone.

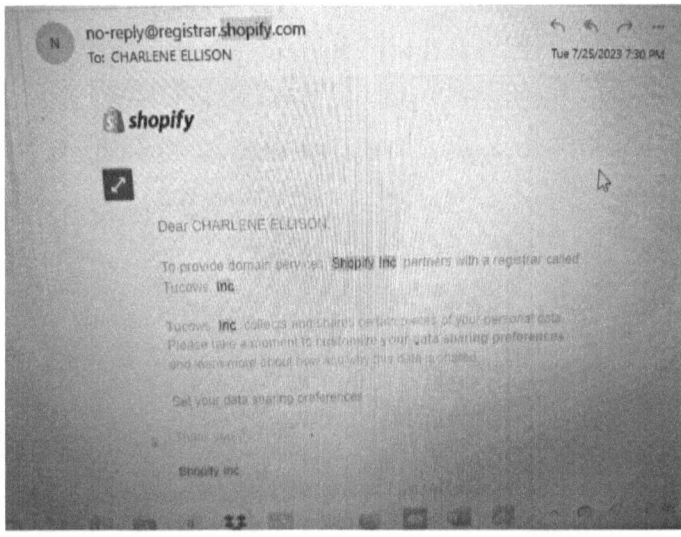

The supplier sent the above email to me stating where to locate their support team when you can clearly see "orders" have clearly been removed from the left side panel. It can be placed and removed if you are not keeping an eye on your store. I had a conversation with Shopify support at one time asking you takes the money when the sale is made, and it startled the individual. The person stated, we take it as well as the supplier can take it as well.

I went to the online stores to try to look for something that I had missed. I noticed I received a message from Shopify on both stores stating the CNAME servers had been changed and my store is not pointing towards them. The stores are pointing to SendGrid, and I do not have an account there. I did not change it. The reason they could not fix it was because my store would have had to pause for 24-48 hours (about 2 days) to populate (turning my store off). I was curious about my server, and I went to google to search DNS lookup. I entered both stores one at a time and received the same IP address utilizing MX Tool DNS Lookup. What triggered Shopify sending the email is that I was able to place Zendesk on the stores which allows graph / analysis and gives me a webhook. Currently both stores have been transferred to a different server against my will and have been stealing from me.

# CNAME notification

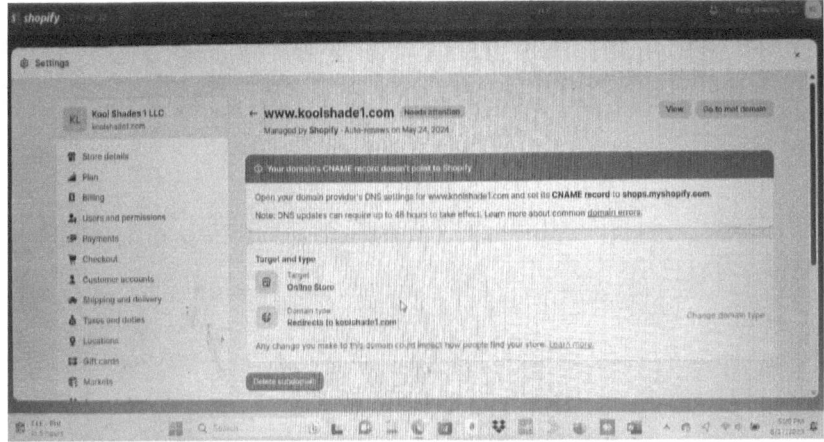

CNAME pointed at SendGrid not Shopify

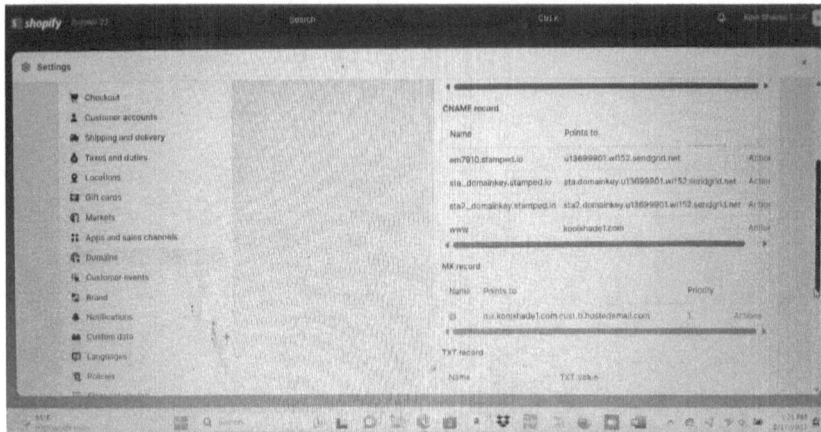

| Name | Points to | |
|------|-----------|---|
| **em7910.stamped.io** | u13699901.wl152.sendgrid.net | Actions |
| **sta._domainkey.stamped.io** | sta.domainkey.u13699901.wl152.sendgrid.net | |

I do not have an account with SendGrid so I looked online on Google to research and reached out to SendGrid via email. No response back. It was somewhat shocking that what happened next almost gave me a panic attack. I was informed that in order for the store to return back to Shopify it would take 24-48 hours (about 2 days) to populate yet it was like Shopify flicked a switch and the store was the back to Shopify less than 10 minutes (very strange)!

## MxToolbar

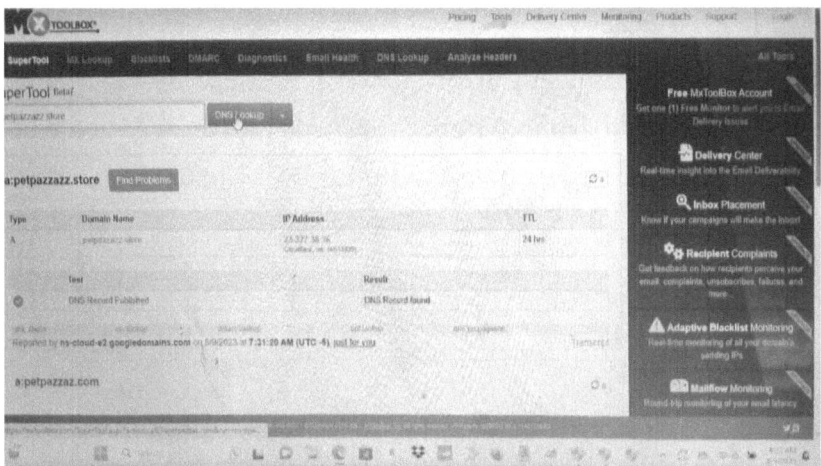

The Mx Tool Bar is significant in understanding if your domain is/was blacklisted, DNS lookup, and IP address as well as other valuable information. Why is this important to a new store owner or a person who needs a better understanding of their store? Your store could be running, and you are unaware of deceptive individuals covering up your over business.

As a result, I sent an email to Shopify legal, and no one contacted me regarding this matter. I explained to them overtime the effect it had on me. This has caused significant damage to me such as anxiety attacks, trauma, defamation of character, racial profiling and affected my ability to trust in having a business due to manipulation. This is a form of fraud, abuse of power, deceit, unlawful and malicious intent. My business is registered through the IRS as an MBR. Although, I reached out to attorneys it seems to be a conflict in issue or they would rather have a class act where it affected several individuals instead of one person. Although, I was advised that if a pursue against me would warrant an investigation against Shopify.

The support message I received when I asked for corporate number. Shopify support stated they don't have one. So, who allows employees to just do every and anything in a company?

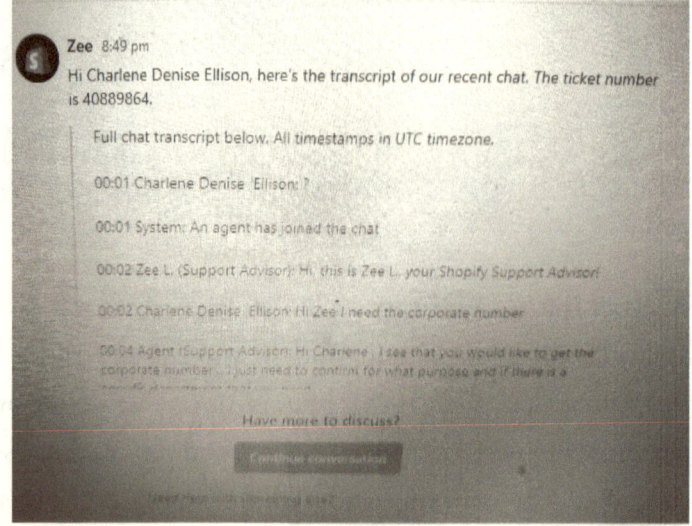

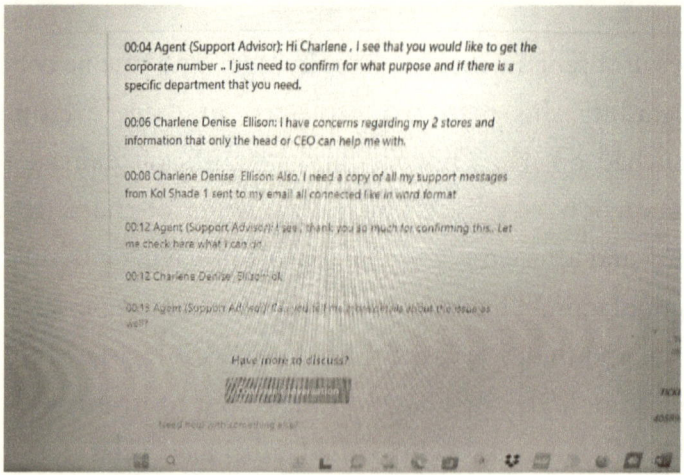

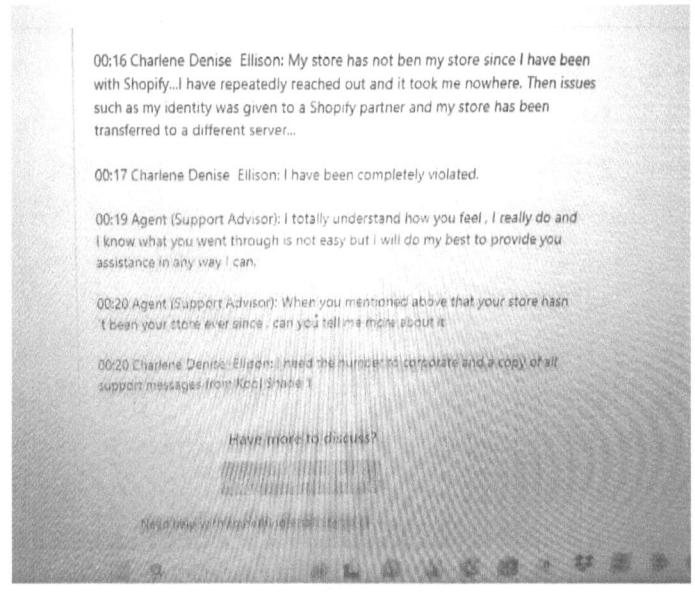

00:16 Charlene Denise Ellison: My store has not ben my store since I have been with Shopify...I have repeatedly reached out and it took me nowhere. Then issues such as my identity was given to a Shopify partner and my store has been transferred to a different server...

00:17 Charlene Denise Ellison: I have been completely violated.

00:19 Agent (Support Advisor): I totally understand how you feel , I really do and I know what you went through is not easy but I will do my best to provide you assistance in any way I can.

00:20 Agent (Support Advisor): When you mentioned above that your store hasn 't been your store ever since , can you tell me more about it

00:20 Charlene Denise Ellison: I need the number to corporate and a copy of all support messages from Kool Shade 1

Have more to discuss?

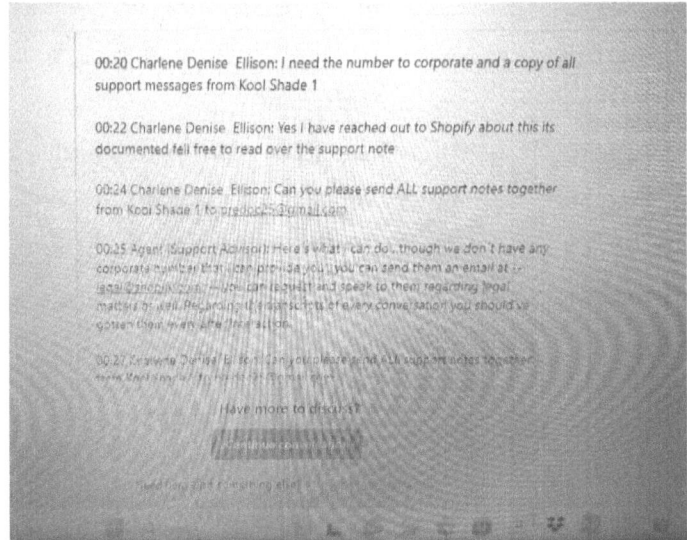

00:20 Charlene Denise Ellison: I need the number to corporate and a copy of all support messages from Kool Shade 1

00:22 Charlene Denise Ellison: Yes I have reached out to Shopify about this its documented fell free to read over the support note

00:24 Charlene Denise Ellison: Can you please send ALL support notes together from Kool Shade 1 to [email]

00:25 Agent (Support Advisor): Here's what I can do , though we don't have any corporate number that I can provide you , you can send them an email at

Have more to discuss?

This has been occurring without the duration of having the Shopify store. I am going to change the server back to Shopify. Also, I am going to look for an attorney of Ecommerce to oversee / manage my stores. I have had a tremendous loss.

Update: I am waiting for a response from, legal@myshopify.com and I decided to delete the store connected to my store. When I deleted it, I went to the site to see this **https://suecf9munzblytei-78275772720.shopifypreview.com**. The reason is that when I changed the DNS to the correct CNAME to point to the store it takes 24-48 hours (about 2 days) for a store to populate so this shows up.

There is a very important reason why this is repeated that will shock you! I want you to look at the picture below in the blue lower right corner. It has a pop up like upsell meaning the store is up and running for Pet Pazzazz as well as taking orders. However, if you look closely at the address, it states Shopify preview in which I had no idea that this store EVER existed. Also, there was another sign stating EUR and I Googled it for international currency. So, now I am like this is like embezzlement white collar crime if this occurring to millions of individuals. It's not their character that they don't care, but it shows my character if I do not make this public in which it can save other people from going through what I experienced.

Here picture of Pet Pazzazz with blue LR
Picture of Kool Shade 1
Picture of amount from Kool Shades 1

Nonetheless Pet Pazzazz is still continuing to be running and Kool Shades 1 is currently frozen. However, I started both stores with a purpose and this did not happen by accident. At the beginning I stated I had previous stores before and it was suspect, yet I had no proof. I honestly felt as if I was racially targeted by racial profiling as an African American woman who was perhaps easily to manipulate and not smart enough to know what was going on. I must admit the first few stores I was actually dumbfounded and taken advantage of by Shopify. But what they did not know was these two stores were intentionally opened and I was paying very close detail to everything that was going on.

My stores were set up from the beginning not to receive payout from either store. I had realized what was going on and decided to just go with the flow. I had to respond to the support to allow them to continue to let me think that everything was alright and once Shopify even went as far as to hang up on me, because I addressed an issue that was quite disturbing. I had to back down and wait for them to become careless with their actions. Consequently, their mistakes started to happen one after another and it almost seemed as if in desperation to how much I knew as well as how much I could prove. Unfortunely, their first mistake was racial profiling me and not knowing that that I was more than I let on.

I want to give you my background so that you can understand why I felt my character was literally attacked. I was a certified nursing assistant for nine years. I wanted to improve my lifestyle, so I went to Remington College and became an occupational therapist assistant in 2017 (GPA 4.0). I decided in my 2$^{nd}$ year to pursue my bachelor's degree in liberal studies (attending 2 different universities at the same time) graduated in 2018 (GPA 3.88) from Purdue University Global. I was so proud of my accomplishments that I enrolled for my master's in psychology graduated in 2020 (3.76) at Purdue University Global. I took time out for myself because due to family matters. I attended Grand Canyon University for one year for my doctorate studies (GPA 3.88) and took time out for my health issues (January 2023). I completed Statistic 1 and 2 my final grade was 98 averages. During the time I wrote cases studies, my master's thesis was published, and I learned various ways to research as well as to investigate. My background I wanted to elaborate on how individuals can be attacked by profiling, and I wanted to give information that can assist you in knowing if you're being scammed or facing an unjust situation.

However, the knowledge I acquired throughout attending school assisted me in how to problem solve and use various methods for research. Unfortunately, my plans are do I keep the stores even though I went through such a horrific experience or do I just terminate them. Shopify would like to terminate it, because that would be the easiest way to get rid of the situation. However, when you have a store with them you can choose to become independent with no affiliation through them, but mindful that their connection must be 100% discontinued or the cycle will continue. I will list information that will assist your store and if it is blocked by them (meaning it is their Shopify app or other app utilizes them) your store could be potentially compromised.

Things To Do To Prior To Opening

Research Niche/product to sell (Google what's 10 top selling products & it gives annual revenue)

IRS/LLC (Free): apply LLC hereeee

Ecommerce store: web developers (creativity and functioning appropriate) near you/ Fiverr, Upwork, and SEOclerks

Ecommerce attorney: Internet Law (helps build credible business)

Data Breach

E-commerce

Domain Disputes

Privacy / Data Breach

Defamation

Inventory app: Keep all products verified within your store

QuickBooks Ecommerce: List and manage products / finances

AI: allows search for traffic when starting your store for products description to be easily recognized by customers

Funnel: upsells (beginning, middle and checkout)

Mail Champ: email messages, graphs and so much more

Speed booster / Optimizer

Place Zendesk: also include webhook (Fiverr / Seoclerks setup inexpensive)

Canvas: product picture/templates, power points, and video

Product Review: Customer reviews

Google GA4: analysis and chart

Multilingual app: English, Spanish, etc.

No need to worry if you can't get the ecommerce attorney just document your store and place all the necessary analysis on it. I did reach out to an attorney, and I received some valuable information for next year on changes that will occur concerning corporate businesses.

The Corporate Transparency Act takes effect on January 1, 2024 (Gordon Law Group). Under the new law, any business defined as a "reporting entity" will need to file reports with FinCEN identifying the beneficial owners of the entity (Gordon Law Group). An individual or company who violates these reporting requirements can be subject to civil penalties up to $10,000, 2 years in prison, or both (Gordon Law Group).

# INTRODUCTION

In the world we live in today, people are filled with greed, power, and how can they take from others. It is really sad when you are a geniune good person and want to do things the right way. I did this book to bring awareness because Gang stalking is real and unfortunately, I was a victim. Gang stalking or group - stalking is a set of persecutory beliefs in which those affected believe they are being followed, stalked, and harrassed ba a large number of people (Google.com). People take this lightly but it actually can be devasting for people physically, emotionally, and mentally. These individuals come to you as good genuine people that have your best interest at heart when really they have a motive the entire time. Have you every heard that we live amongst people with smiling faces yet they have the uglist hearts. There is light and dark in which sometimes it is good to have experienced both, because one day the intuition, dream or instincts can reduce alot of unneccesary pain. If you are around someone and they make you uncomfortable follow your gut or a particular situation trust that feeling!

I want to elaborate on how abuse of power can be in a workplace, local businesses, and online due to an unjust advantage. I have encountered several opportunities that I thought would add to my life yet it subtracted and left me in a position that I would not even wish on my enemy. I want to give a preview before we dive into the specific details of each company and the reasons I am exposing them. Many people use Shopify to make online sales and purchases throughout the day. There are countless number of people that have benefited from Shopify and then there are people who never really got to tell their story. My story can help others, because sometimes people don't know what to do. I believe knowledge is power, because it teaches others and reduces bad cycles from continuing.

Quick Fix Tech Solutions was a devastating job in which I believed that this company was ethical and I would have a sense of job security, However, the nightmare suddenly happened and the faces changed to the actual people I did not see at the beginning. I don't wan to spoil the details with facts and recipts for all companies so the book is not opinated. I will tell you my experience at the beginning was like a fairy tale and some would think I made it all up, but this storyline is going to blow your MIND!

I moved on to Full Credit Sweep in which of course they repair your credit. I thought to myself this is going to be a great experience and I can achieve a high credit score. Unfortunately, I went to through 2 months and it is still ongoing of pure hell, poor customer service, and abuse of power at it's finest. There is so much to speak on when it comes to this company so I won't spoil the news just yet.....but wait there's so much more to go.

Now, I'm starting a new employment, I am going in with a positive attidude and I am on a 30 -day probationary period. So, at the beginning I was like this is not hard and just make sure the rules are followed. Oh, by the way the company is Amazon Delivery Services LLC. The company is a third party affiliate that is under the radar as a hit and miss. The earned hit and miss due to the severity of what occurred in just a short time frame. I can't wait until you see what occured.

The present company is relatively was concurrent with the Amazon Delivery Services, so I dont want you to confuse the two companies. Cargill Shipping is a company that provide services to the USA and international customers. They have so many team leads and rules that would make you think this company has it all together, but don't get your hopes up too high they are a crooked as can be... I will indeed bring reciepts, texts, and emails throughout majority of the this book. This will seem as if I have lost my mind as I tell my truth and unveil the darkside of these companies.

I am now at the last one and I promise you I can't make this up. My experience is at Regions Bank in a small town in Gainesville, Florida. The case is ongoing for nearly 2 months now and has been a complete nightmare. My mindset was that banks should be a safe place in which people use their services and for me it was the complete opposite. Well, I know you are thinking it could not get any worse.... wait until you see what it is as of 7/17/2024 it is not business as usual, but rather win, lose or draw.

These book is based off of real life events that will have you questioning people's intentions and wondering why I did not lose my mind while going through the process. I wanted so much to go to social media to speak my mind, but it would have did nothing but set me back due to some companies are ongoing. People everyday face issues and they go through situations that changes them. Some individuals let things go with the "that's life" phrase and that allow these companies to continue to abuse their power. No one wants to be a victim, no one wants to look like a so called snitch, but nothing changes unless people are held accountable for thier actions and that is why I am their walking Karma!

I was initially advised to be very careful, because these business could retaliate and my safety for exposing them. I have no fear of what they could possibly do to me, because I speak facts and I was handled in a way that not only violated my rights, but changed me as a person. I fought so hard for what I wanted and it was the very thing that I needed to let go. Life humbles us when we are on a pedistal and that was not my life. My life was simple while working to achieve goals, and people saw that as an opportunity to knock me down further. When I say it was God who kept me sane, and that is why I cannot stop because of my faith. People don't understand.... You can't break a person who gets their strength from God (Alli Worthington)!

# SCAMMED BY SHOPIFY

See the attachment in the book
Shopify
151 O'Conner Street
Ground floor, Ottawa, ON K2P 2L8

# QUICK FIX TECH SOLUTIONS

I was going through a rough time in life and facing health issues so I was like I wanted to work from home. The job market was hard due to people wanted you either to have experience, was not hiring, or if you meet their qualifications. I felt as though I was very humble, but simply over qualified for alot of jobs that was not interested. I did not feel discouraged and I continued to have the faith that I would find a job that was compatible. I went online to Part-Time Recruiters and applied for a work from home position. Days went by then finally I recieved a call for 2 interviews. I was offered a position for Regional Manager at Quick Fix Tech Solutions.

I had to start the training, but my job offer came with bonuses and I was very excited. Intially, the job training was conducted from Slack and it was not hard work but a set schedule. I had to open up 6 bank accounts for three businesses, but only 3 businesses was being used at that time. I thought that okay it's a slow process, then the money started to come into the account at $10,000 and more. But then, I waited two months and I was excited about buying a car and I specifically wanted a used car. The first flag some people would have been the six bank accounts, but then the company offered me shares when the business ends. I would say the first flag was actually going to the dealer and they asked me how long I worked there, because my taxes was not adding up. My paperwork what was holding me back and then I was like how I never noticed that from the beginning.

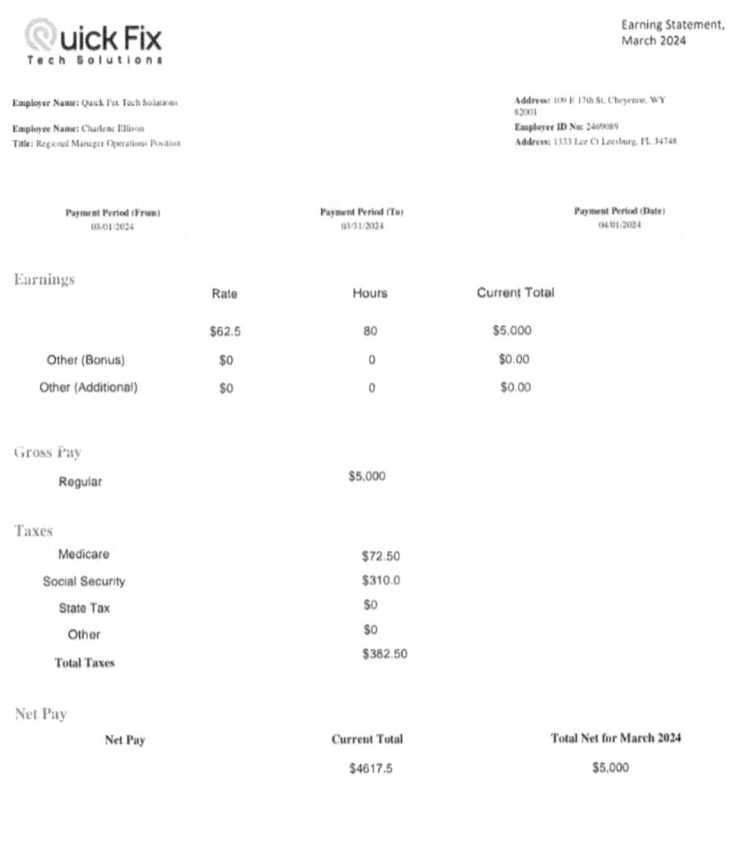

## uick Fix
### Tech Solutions

Earning Statement,
March 2024

**Employer Name:** Quick Fix Tech Solutions

**Employer Name:** Charlene Ellison
**Title:** Regional Manager Operations Position

**Address:** 109 E 17th St, Cheyenne, WY 82001
**Employee ID No:** 2469089
**Address:** 1333 Lee Ct Leesburg, FL 34748

| Payment Period (From) 03/01/2024 | Payment Period (To) 03/31/2024 | Payment Period (Date) 04/01/2024 |
| --- | --- | --- |

**Earnings**

| | Rate | Hours | Current Total |
| --- | --- | --- | --- |
| | $62.5 | 80 | $5,000 |
| Other (Bonus) | $0 | 0 | $0.00 |
| Other (Additional) | $0 | 0 | $0.00 |

**Gross Pay**

| | |
| --- | --- |
| Regular | $5,000 |

**Taxes**

| | |
| --- | --- |
| Medicare | $72.50 |
| Social Security | $310.0 |
| State Tax | $0 |
| Other | $0 |
| **Total Taxes** | $382.50 |

**Net Pay**

| Net Pay | Current Total | Total Net for March 2024 |
| --- | --- | --- |
| | $4617.5 | $5,000 |

**Note:** This is a computer generated Invoice and does not require a signature.

I contacted my supervisor repeatedly for my bonuses and everytime it was brushed to the side as if you should be happy with what you have now. I am very appreciative, but I would like what is rightfully owed to me. I had to handle different bank interactions / transitions and had encountered a weird interaction with Bank of America. They had placed a hold on the bank account. The department was the Takeover Department in which they was hanging up, transferring me, and went as far as to say if they give the money back. They actually thought they were going to keep the money. I waited 2-3 weeks constantly calling and the bank released the money via UPS for signing. Immediately, after that I went to $5,000 a month. I must admit I had priviledge of using the card yet it came out of my income. I let the bonus situation go at that time and focused on the here and now.

Everything was going smootly and the business running smoothly. Then I recieved a call from the company who interviewed me and I mentioned the bonuses to them and they were like you haven't recieved a bonus yet. So, we both are sitting there shocked and I decided to talk to my supervisor as well as the HR department. IT was interesting to me that we had reached the over $300,000 and I was looked over everytime for the bonus. Everyone was brushing me to the side and my supervisor stated one day that its only on special occassions and there are none. Wow, a slap in the face because she didn't know I spoke with the hiring department. So, at that moment I put it together and realized my bonuses were occuring, but I was not getting them. Then, I started to feel like a fool while looking for another employment.

After that, I asked around another 2 weeks and it was shut down with no converstaion. So, I reached out to my supervisor and told her that they are like around $400,000 and the greed would still not allow them to pay the bonus. I went to the bank took at my pay plus an additional $5000 which was not a big bonus but it was the right amount from Google. I recieved a call and my supervisor and I talked as I continued to work. I had a family emergency I went out of town for 5 days and took the laptop so that I can work. Upon, returning home it was business as usual. Everything was stated it was fine, because we had communicated. Then, I recieve an email stating that the money needs to be put back a week later. I thought of it and said it's not worth it and allowed them to replace with the check. Then, all of a sudden I noticed changes and I was like wait....what's going on.

The Chase Bank was overdrowned $1,900 and Trusit Bank overdrowned $900. So, then I reached out to them in regards to a negative account.So, I reached out to them and they waiting for a deposit, but little did I know the last 2-3 weeks was them transitioning. Then, when it was time for me to recieve pay I did not recieve it. So, I actually started to think even though the business accounts was closed down the websites were still up and running and they were not paying by using my name. Now, I'm realizing I have another issue on my hand, but I knew I had to focus on finding other employment due to their lack of appreciation of my dedication and hard work.

https://www.edudexsolutions.com
https://www.visionsoltech.com

But doing the process the Slack remains open, but I do not communicate with anyone. Because I was too smart for my own good that I started realizing too much and then they had to wonder how much do she know? I started frequently having doubts and IRS anxiety that I started to ask questions, but they were not fully answered. Like I previously stated the job was like as fairy tale and then it became a nightmare because I have unfinish business to resolve with them. The power of greed and then to take on someone's identity as you are me is beyond delusional. When the whole time I was having a heart they were actually sitting back laughing because their plan was working for awhile. Oh well, I guess all good things come to an end, but unfortunately for them not the way they intended.

Quick Fix Tech Solutions
Sandra Wilson
109 E. 17th Street
Cheyenne, Wyoming 82001
302-440-1509

# FULL CREDIT SWEEP

Everyone wants to find a business that say what they mean and provide the necessary plan to get there. I must admit that the plan was laid out and with four steps then everything was ready to start. Unfortunately, I was just starting a new job and that was a month away and I asked for the $700 refund back. I explained to the cutomer service why I needed it back and I would return when financially set. At first, I was like this is going to be a smooth transaction with no worries due to they did not perform any work. I was mistaken about the hit and miss company.

May 3, 1:39 PM

Conversation with (718) 568-5027

Hey Charlene, we're reaching out to you from the Dispute Team at Full Credit Sweep.

We're very excited to help take your credit score to new heights!

Please follow the link below to upload the necessary documents in order to verify your identity with the credit bureaus:

https://en.fullcreditsweep.com/onboarding/

Once you complete this step, follow the link below to add positive credit history on your credit profile. (Free)

https://en.fullcreditsweep.com/free-credit-boost/

After completing the steps above, you'll be able to keep track of your disputes as well as your progress at anytime through your Client Dashboard.

Please text "Help" if you need additional assistance in uploading these files.

Thank you for choosing us as your

📎   Send message

Days turned into endless text messages and calls wondering why the refund had not been recieved weeks later. I was reassurred that is was escalated to a higher department and no need to worry. I started to think which card did it go on, because they maybe the issue due to the card was no longer active. But I was reassured by the bank the money would not enter the account due to it's closed. Then I started going through my messages and was like this is way too much. I went to Google and searched Full Credit Sweep number and spoke with someone in the sales department. My first call was with Mark Smith, who completed a ticket, and asked me to take his number to find out where the account was at the present time. He told me that my account had not information that was visable to him and it was locked so he could not see what was going on. He asked me to give him two days and I called back with no answer from him. I waited a few days to call back and it is being endorsed waiting for a manager's response.

Then, I started calling the customer service assigned to me and it was going to voicemail. She was no longer answering my calls or answering texts. Now, it has been close to two months and I have accomplished absolutely nothing with them. I decided to contact sales again I reached a different individual who placed a ticket and asked me to wait 24-48 hours before customer service to call. Well, I waited the timeframe and no one has returned my call. So, what is the gameplan now, I make another call to get an update. When I call I recieve text messages when the calls do not go through.

← (718) 568-5027  ⋮

May 23, 12:47 PM

 Hey Charlene, hope all is well!

Sorry we missed your call, one of our specialized agents will be reaching out to you shortly ☎

You may also reply to this text message with the reason for your call and one of our live agents will help.

Hey Charlene, hope all is well!

Sorry we missed your call, one of our specialized agents will be reaching out to you shortly ☎

You may also reply to this text message with the reason for your call and one of our live agents will help.

I am calling to receive an update on my refund

I'm reporting this I'm calling the main office.

May 24, 10:33 AM

 Hey Charlene, hope all is well!

 Send message

Are credit sweeps are illegal? King Credit Services speaks on credit sweeps on a TikTok video (Google.com). I was excited about what they offered without actualy doing the research (Google.com). Unfortunately for many unsuspecting consumers looking to improve their credit, the credit sweep is a fradulent and illegal practice (Google.com). John Ulzheimer, one of the nations most prominent credit experts, explains why you need to watch out for credit sweep scams in an episode of Credit Countdown (Google.com). I am like amazed at how many companies are offering credit sweeps and was curious from the begining how they were able to get it comleted. Now, I have a better understanding of what occurred, not everything glitters is gold and I will not be moving forward with there services after what I experienced with them. I believe my experiences can help others because I am speaking in truth and with proof. I continued to reach out to Angie in support and she stopped responding to text messages around 6/20/2024.

I recieved a call from Don Keller in the sales department. He stated he was calling regarding my account on 7/19/2024. I told him that I have been going through the process for over two months. He said, he's not in the blaming game, but on how to resolve this issue. I explained that it happened to me not him. He asked to check my text message for Ashley Cruze from support who will be assising me. The original support did absolutely nothing to get this resolved. Immediately, after I thanked him I left a message for Ashley Cruze and left a message on the website stating they will reach out within 24 hours. No one has contacted me and I have left several messages on the phone and website. As far as my refund, I am still calling and texting so I can close this chapter.

I recieved a call from Don Keller in the sales department. He stated he was calling regarding my account on 7/19/2024. I told him that I have been going through the process for over two months. He said, he's not in the blaming game, but on how to resolve this issue. I explained that it happened to me not him. He asked to check my text message for Ashley Cruze from support who will be assising me. The original support did absolutely nothing to get this resolved. Immediately, after I thanked him I left a message for Ashley Cruze and left a message on the website stating they will reach out within 24 hours. No one has contacted me and I have left several messages on the phone and website. As far as my refund, I am still calling and texting so I can close this chapter.

7 hours ago, 2:29 PM

Hello Charlene,

As mentioned previously, we have forwarded your concern to our Billing Department along with your card details, and we are currently awaiting their response. Regarding our previous attempt, the transaction did not go through, and our funds are still pending. Being a smaller company, we rely on our merchant to release these funds, which can sometimes cause delays.

If you had requested a reversal on the same day you signed up, we could have initiated it promptly. However, we were waiting for your updates regarding sending your documents. Understandably, you mentioned encountering financial difficulties, which further delayed the process. Therefore, please understand that the funds we are attempting to reverse are still in a pending status.

Thank you for your patience and understanding in this matter.

Hello Charlene,

As mentioned previously, we have forwarded your concern

📎   Send message

I had talked with Angie Reyes from support. I asked for billing phone number or email address and she stated all calls are completed through customer service support or sales. She stated that the billing funds are on hold by the merchant and that's why I haven't received the money, but before I have been told repeatedly that money is being processed back to the card. This is the last text that I sent to them on 7/30/2024. Then I reached back out to let them know how unaccepatble this is and they are doing bad business on 8/07/24 as well as give me MY MONEY!

call and one of our live agents will help.

I am calling I want my money

Yesterday, 4:21 PM

 Hey Charlene, hope all is well!

Sorry we missed your call, one of our specialized agents will be reaching out to you shortly ☎

You may also reply to this text message with the reason for your call and one of our live agents will help.

Where is my money? I want my money now!

I going to post this all over Social media

 Hello Charlene, we are still waiting for our funds to return. We are also waiting. Please understand we already informed you about the issue we have with our merchant. We sincerely apologize for the delays and for the inconvenience and we appreciate your patience.

📎 Send message

Full Credit Sweep
1-877-805-1197
No address provided

# AMAZON DELIVERY SERVICES LLC

After placing numerous applications online, I was contacted by Amazon Delivery Services LLC and I had to take an entrance test to accept the job. I passed the test and signed an E-doc for the offer letter to accept the job. I was like okay I have to go into this job with a new mind set, because this is a different company RIGHT! The human resource contacted me and assigned a supervisor to me (Daniel Sam) and his supervisor (Hanna Kaminski). He made several contacts with me via email, phone calls, and text messages. At first, I was a little skeptical due to having to wait a time period for my 1st pakage and it arrived and I was like this is legit. I recieved a bar code label to submit and send the package off to the designated carrier. I was like okay this is easy work for a short-time frame for $2400 working for the month. I went in to the job knowing that is was on a 30-day probationary period.

**Alan Gray** May 21

to me ⌄

Dear Charlene,

Welcome to our team! It's a pleasure to have you on board.

Let's dive into some essential details. As outlined in your Employment Agreement, your 30-day probation period begins from the second shipment. This date will be visible in the Task Control System under Profile - Payment Data - Payday. Subsequent payday dates will also be displayed there.

For your probation month, you will earn a base rate of $2000, $85.00 for transport expenses, and bonuses for each task.

We have a few perks for you:

Occasionally, you may incur job-related expenses for items like clear packing tape, ink cartridges, a basic printer, etc. You can be reimbursed for these products by emailing copies of your receipts to the Payroll Department. You can submit them individually or all at once at the end of your probation.

Reimbursement for job-related expenses, as well as a fixed gas reimbursement, will be added to your first paycheck without the need to attach receipts for gas.

Now, let's discuss the necessary documentation to ensure smooth and timely processing of your paycheck.

Your first payment during the probationary period will be processed on an Independent Contractor basis with no tax deductions. To facilitate this, please complete the enclosed IRS W-9 tax form. Your earnings must be reported to the IRS at the end of the year. Return the completed form to me within three days of starting your probation to avoid delays in releasing your paycheck.

Please note that we only accept electronic submission of documents via email, as regular mail cannot guarantee the security of sensitive information. Our email correspondence is encrypted and remains highly secure.

Your first paycheck will be a regular paper check and will be mailed at the end of your training (30 days after the second

# Job Description

Remote Assistant

## Structure

1. Company's profile
2. Remote assistant role
3. Duties
4. Requirements for the candidates
5. Employment terms
6. Salary
7. How to apply

## Company's profile

| | |
|---|---|
| **Legal Name:** | Amazon Delivery Services LLC |
| **Legal Address:** | 820 Federal School Ln, New Castle, DE 19720 |
| **EIN:** | 99-1366614 |
| **State File ID:** | 3161821 (Delaware) |
| **Website:** | https://amazondservices.com/ |

Our company specializes in preparing goods for shipment to clients on FBA Amazon or other trading platforms. Many of our clients are arbitrage sellers who purchase items in stores and resell them on Amazon. For these sellers, efficient and high-quality preparation of products for sale is crucial. Maintaining a warehouse can be costly, which is why many sellers utilize the services of companies like ours.

We provide professional and reliable service, ensuring that customers receive their products promptly and in excellent condition. Additionally, we help sellers avoid any potential issues that may arise from violating delivery terms. Our company guarantees that all products will arrive at their destination without loss or damage and within the shortest possible time frame.

## Remote Assistant role

As a Remote Assistant, your responsibilities include receiving and checking the commodities of our arbitrage sellers, preparing them for shipping, and shipping them to either the general warehouse or the customers of our clients. It is crucial that you inspect the incoming goods promptly, prepare them for shipping, and ship them with the provided shipping labels to the destination point.

At our company, we operate under a decentralized control mode, which means that our employees process our clients' goods remotely. This approach allows us to expedite the workflow and reduce expenses for storage, transportation, and warehouse maintenance. Additionally, our employees the flexibility to work from home according to their convenience.

We prioritize the interests of customers who seek reliable delivery of their purchased good collaborate with sellers by offering transportation services for their commodities to custo. Customers pay us for high-quality service, and when a package is delivered, the seller receives payment for the commodity. While we work with a diverse range of sellers, the key points of our company's operations remain consistent:

- Commodities and packaging safety during transportation

46

My packages were very slow to come, so I said this is a great opportunity that turns into increase pay and I wanted to think positive about the situation. They say "a negative mind will not give you a positive life (Ziad K. Abdelnour)." I did not start recieving packages until the 2nd week. I recieved 2 packages and then 2 more packages towards the end. I reached out to my assistant supervisor and asked if this correct or should I be recieving more packages. He told me not to worry, because everyone goes through this before becoming a full-time employee. I was content knowing I did what was required following there rules. Here is a picture of a merchandisor box that was extremely heavy.

Okay, now I am bringing you up to date with my probationary period has ended and I am waiting for the pay check. I waited a week because of the July 4th Independence day. I emailed the payroll department stating that I did not receive the check. I told him was important that I get paid or it could possible place me in financial hardship. I reached to human resource, and both supervisor's no response. I kept reaching out and then realized how they had did me! At first, I was angry and upset, because I did everything they asked me to do. Then, there was no reason to get that mad, because I needed a level head in moving forward with a strategic plan. I lose my cool then I lose everything and they win. Here is a message from my supervisor Sam reassuring me I will get paid.

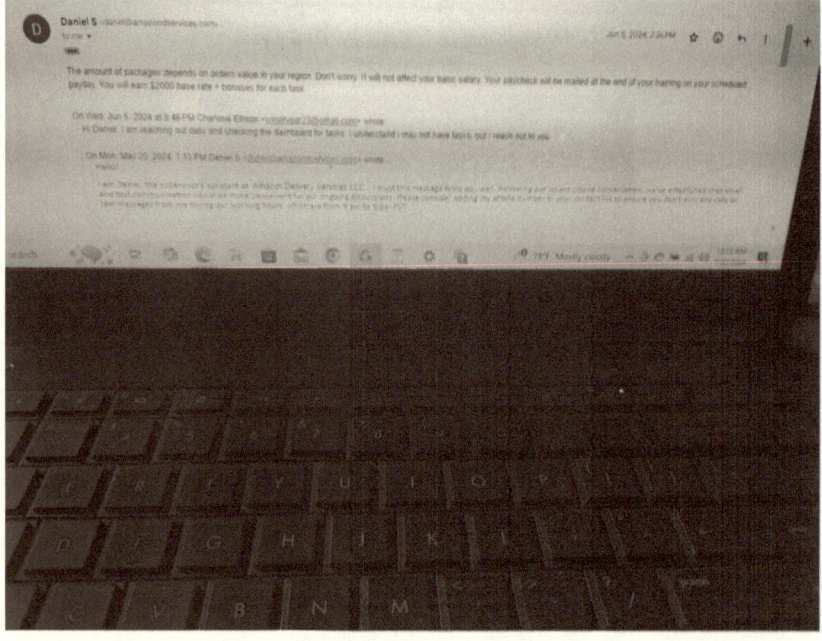

The writing is small it states: The amount of packages depends on orders value in your region. Don't worry. It will not affect your basic salary. Your paycheck will be mailed at the end of your training on your scheduled payday. You will earn $2000 base rate + bonuses for each task.

This is the image of where the packages were shipped to the customers.

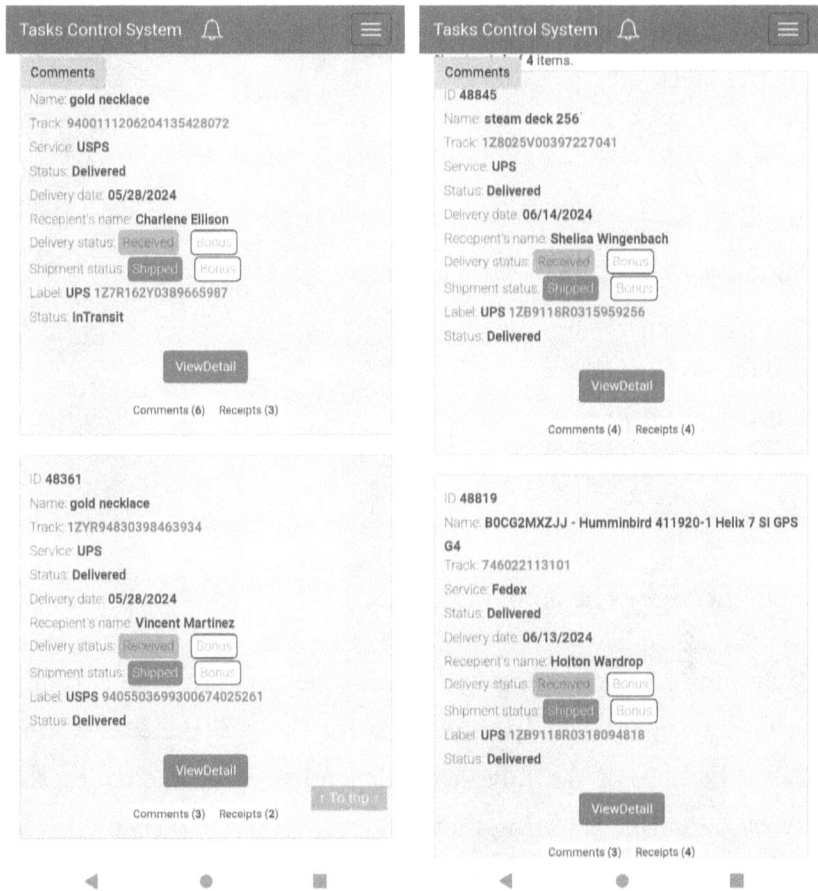

Now, I am currently in the stage of acceptance that I was a target from the beginning. Their game plan was to never pay me, but to look as is if they were going to do so. Unfortunately, I did not quit I believed in me that what they did will place them under investigation and they will have to face others who they have victimized. But I love keeping receipts, because it allows a trace and at the end will reveal why this happened and they face the necessary charges.

Eliska Novakova
HR Manager
1-302-947-5855
Alan Gray
Payroll Department
Daniel Sam
Supervisor's assistant
302-386-8182
Hanna Kaminski
Direct Supervisor
303-278-0011

Email message- The amount of packages

Okay, now I am bringing you up to date with my probationary period has ended and I am waiting for the pay check. I waited a week because of the July 4th Independence day. I emailed the payroll department stating that I did not receive the check. I told him was important that I get paid or it could possible place me in financial hardship. I reached to human resource, and both supervisor's no response. I kept reaching out and then realized how they had did me! At first, I was angry and upset, because I did everyhting they asked me to do. Then, there was no reason to get that mad, because I needed a level head in moving forward with a strategic plan. I lose my cool then I lose everything and they win. Here is a message from my supervisor Sam reassuring me I will get paid.

The writing is small it states: The amount of packages depends on orders value in your region. Don't worry. It will not affect your basic salary. Your paycheck will be mailed at the end of your training on your scheduled payday. You will earn $2000 base rate + bonuses for each task.

This the statement I recieved from payroll:

Congratulations on completing your probationary period!

Now, I am currently in the stage of acceptance that I was a target from the beginning. Their game plan was to never pay me, but to look as is if they were going to do so. Unfortunately, I did not quit I believed in me that what they did will place them under investigation and they will have to face others who they have victimized. But I love keeping receipts, because it allows a trace and at the end will reveal why this happened and they face the necessary charges.

Eliska Novakova
HR Manager
1-302-947-5855
Alan Gray
Payroll Department
Daniel Sam
Supervisor's assistant
302-386-8182
Hanna Kaminski
Direct Supervisor
303-278-0011

# CARGILL SHIPPING

When I was working with Amazon Delivery Services LLC their was a low package rate and so I started looking for companies similar in sending packages for work. My application was accepted by Cargill Shipping and I went through the process recieving emails, texts, and numerous calls from the employer. I was excited because they offered me a salary of $3000 and bonuses for each package. I was going to run both businesses cocurrent and I was tired some days yet I had bills to pay. I was thinking this is a blessing from God because of the challenges I had been experiencing. I was informed that my packages would come with notification from the shipper and I would also recieve unknown packages at my from door from the warehouse.

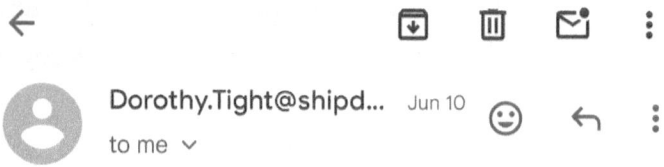

Dorothy.Tight@shipd...   Jun 10

to me ⌄

Dear Charlene,

We're excited to share that your dashboard has been successfully activated. To finalize your setup, please follow these steps:

1. Visit our website: https://cshipping-dash.com/user/ and log in using the username and password you previously created.

2. Upon logging in, navigate to the "HELP" section within the dashboard. We strongly advise thoroughly reviewing this section, as it contains crucial information for your position as an Inspection Specialist. Take the time to download and carefully study the step-by-step instructions provided, complete with useful screenshots.

3. It's important to ensure that my email address is added to your contact list, as you will receive multiple emails from me related to your tasks.

If you come across any inquiries or uncertainties, please don't hesitate to reach out to me. Our team is committed to making your onboarding process seamless.

We extend a warm welcome to our team and wish you great success in your new role.

Best regards,

Shipping Department

**Cargill Shipping**
1 Ace St Unit 12, Fall River, MA 02720
(888) 688-2599

Office Hours: Mon-Fri 09:00AM-06:00PM EST
Sat-Sun Closed

11

Well, now I am booked and busy working very hard recieving around 4-5 packages a week. I was now relieved my stress, because I had constant contact with my supervisor daily, the other supervisor when needed, and the manager to see how well everything was going. I recieved a welcome to the team warm call and I was feeling a sense of security. My guard was completely let down due to I was so busy and I had not experienced any issues while working. In fact, I was constantly recieving calls about how great of a job I am doing and they are pleasesd with my work.

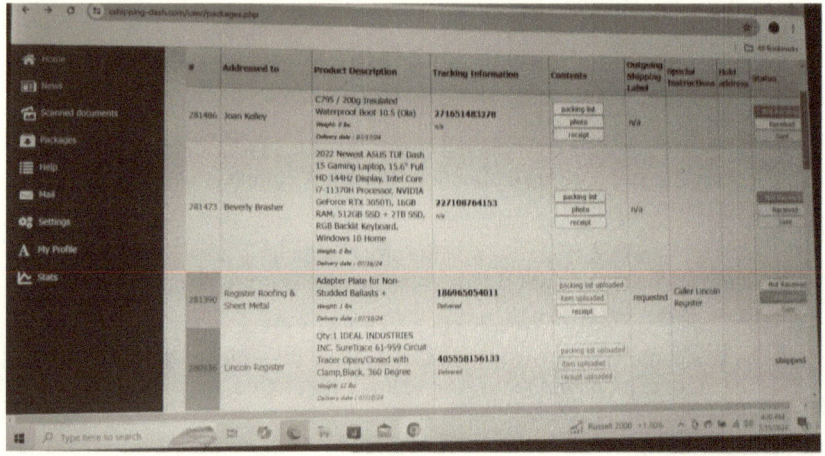

Noted: The above names Joan Kelley was in the process of ordering a waterproof insulated boot and Beverly Brasher was ordering a gaming ipad yet this is the time they placed N/A and the deliveries stopped due to non-payment.

I woke up and recieved a call from Brenda with the purchasing department stating that they are pleased with my work and wanted to offer me a Agent purchasing position with paid training running concurrent with the position I have 3 days a week. She stated I have been very thoural in my work and one of the best employees they have had in awhile. She stated my time management was the reason they wanted to promote me. I was so excited that I could not believe this was happening at 3 weeks into work. The promotion came with a salary of $6000 per month plus bonuses in which was a very big increase from what I was initially offered. But there was a catch to it. I had to have a credit card and they place the money on their to complete the purchases. Well, the idea had me with flash backs of what I experienced with Quick Fix Tech Solutions and I was left with the issues at the end. So, I initially accepted before I knew I needed to have my credit card and I was not comfortable with the position qualifiaction. I would expect a company to have a business credit card for purchasing or to utilize a bank card for the business.

As a result, I did not take the position. It was a choice I made and I was comfortable with the decision. Although, the packages were steady coming in I would like to give an idea of what I was receiving and some required signatures. The packages are not limited but are the following: packages with $100 gift cards, Tesla car parts ($2500-$3000), Lincoln car parts ($2200), iPhone tablet ($1300), and so many more expensive items.

Jun 10, 2:55 PM

Conversation with (754) 310-2798

Congrats! Your account's approved. Log in and explore the "HELP" section at Cshipping Dash. To opt-out, reply "STOP."

New message in your mailbox from Cshipping Dash. To opt-out, reply "STOP."

Jun 11, 9:53 AM

Hey Charlene Ellison, new package added. Check your account at Cshipping Dash. To opt-out, reply "STOP."

Jun 14, 12:10 PM

New message in your mailbox from Cshipping Dash. To opt-out, reply "STOP."

Hey Charlene Ellison, new package added. Check your account at Cshipping Dash. To opt-out, reply "STOP."

Jun 15, 6:33 PM

📎 Send message

...................................
"STOP."

Hi Charlene Ellison, package label (ashland summer rattan pendant light white cord) uploaded. Check your account at Cshipping Dash. To opt-out, reply "STOP."

Hi Charlene Ellison, package label (Pick up - ADVANCE AUTO PARTS STORE 9236 , 1035 E UNIVERSITY AVE , GAINESVILLE, FL , 32601 , US Holder - Weston Herman 505 SW 2nd Ave APT 5205 Gainesville, FL 32601 newegg

1x ASUS TUF Gaming Monitor VG27AQA1A
1x Thermaltake toughpower gf1 750w TT Premium Edition Power Supply
1x  t-force vulcan 32gb (2*16gb) 6000MHz ddr5 kit) uploaded. Check your account at Cshipping Dash. To opt-out, reply "STOP."

Jul 3, 9:36 AM

Hi Charlene Ellison, package label (ipad pro 11-inch m4 wi-fi+cell 256 gb) uploaded. Check your account at Cshipping Dash. To opt-out, reply "STOP."

Send message ➤

You're welcome I will retake it

Also for the Tesla cable do I take a picture of that as well?

Can you please remove the photo on ID278604

Jul 1, 12:37 PM

New message in your mailbox from Cshipping Dash. To opt-out, reply "STOP."

Hey Charlene Ellison, new package added. Check your account at Cshipping Dash. To opt-out, reply "STOP."

Hi Charlene Ellison, package label (2x Tesla Motors 24' Cable Wall Connector) uploaded. Check your account at Cshipping Dash. To opt-out, reply "STOP."

New message in your mailbox from Cshipping Dash. To opt-out, reply "STOP."

Jul 2, 6:32 AM

Send message

58

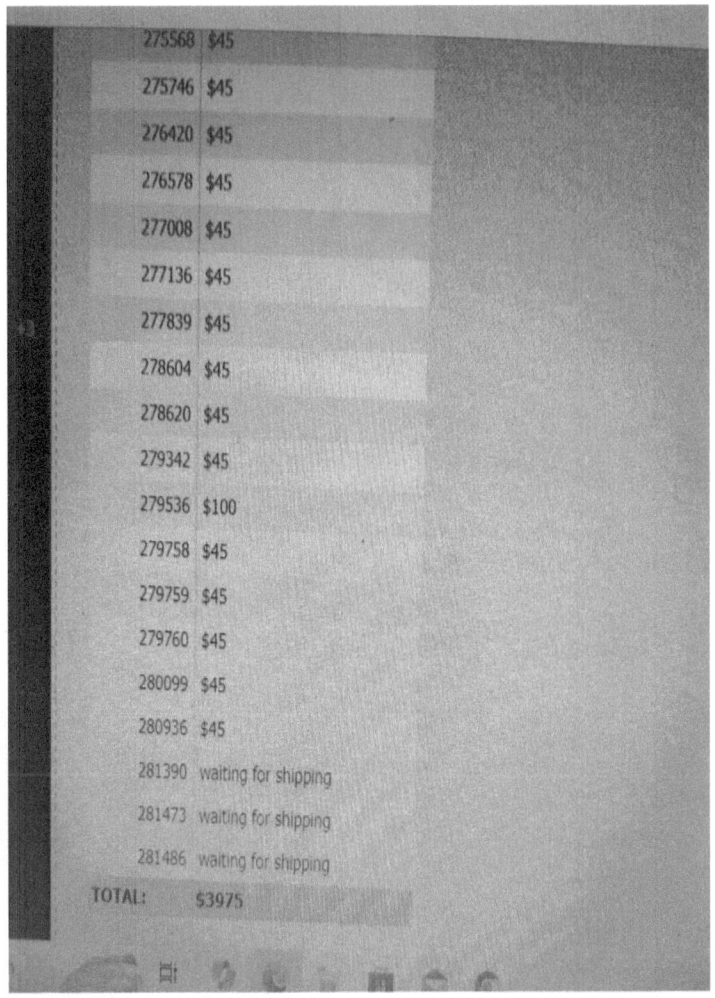

| | |
|---|---|
| 275568 | $45 |
| 275746 | $45 |
| 276420 | $45 |
| 276578 | $45 |
| 277008 | $45 |
| 277136 | $45 |
| 277839 | $45 |
| 278604 | $45 |
| 278620 | $45 |
| 279342 | $45 |
| 279536 | $100 |
| 279758 | $45 |
| 279759 | $45 |
| 279760 | $45 |
| 280099 | $45 |
| 280936 | $45 |
| 281390 | waiting for shipping |
| 281473 | waiting for shipping |
| 281486 | waiting for shipping |
| TOTAL: | $3975 |

The last 3 items two of them was never posted N/A and I kept the last one after they blocked me.

I am now moving towards my ending of the month, because this job pays monthly as well. I had a final package to send out and it came in two boxes in which needed different labels. I delivered the 1st package. In requested a label for the second package. The message below is what I recieved from my work dashboard.

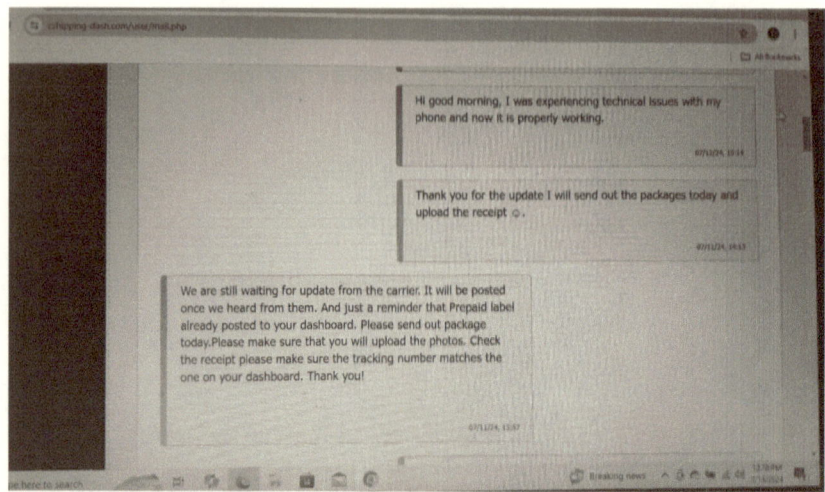

This is the last package that was sent out:

Circuit Tracker cost $2,036.74 to Jacksonville, Florida.

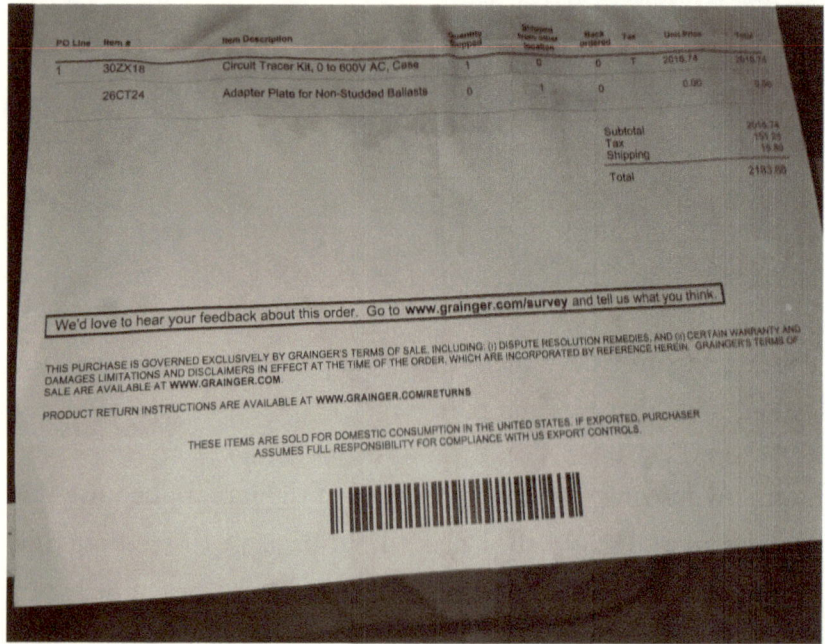

In the account team email all packages will be sent out during the 30th and 31st day, then release of direct deposit. What they did was not send the label for the last package after I did the following: sent an email, text message, placed message in work dashboard, and called them. I recieved a message they were waiting for the customer to fufill the label on 7/11/2024. Also, they added two more packages with no delivery dates. I went into the account to check for a label and follow protocol for 3 x a day check in. When I went to sign in on 7/17/2024 the account stated wrong password 3x and they blocked me.

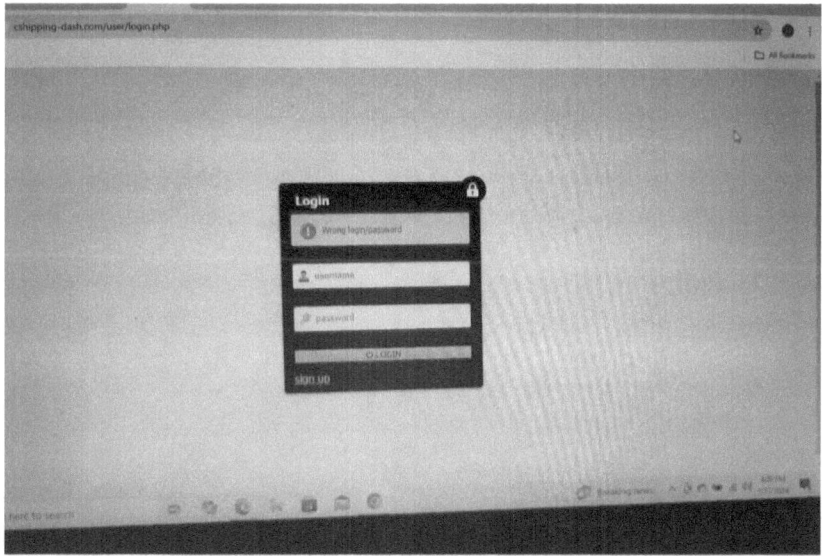

My direct deposit it was four days and I did not recieve it. I contacted accounting, purchasing department, supervisor's and manager. I recieved NO response from anyone. I called each one followed by emails and texts. Now, I am starting to panic having extreme anxiety and don't know what to do. I mean everything that was required I did it and I am basically at the beginning with nothing to show for it. I am now at the filing of the eviction stage for my apartment from the manager. I am at this point very disapointed, because I didn't steal or not do my job and I faced abuse of power as well wage theft for the 2nd time placing me pratically homeless. I paid for ride share to deliver the packages and print out labels at the store for both delivery services. Also, I had a couple in Gainesville who assisted me in delivering packages and I had to explain to them what was going on and I felt like a horrible person, because now I included individuals in this who was waiting to recieve payment.

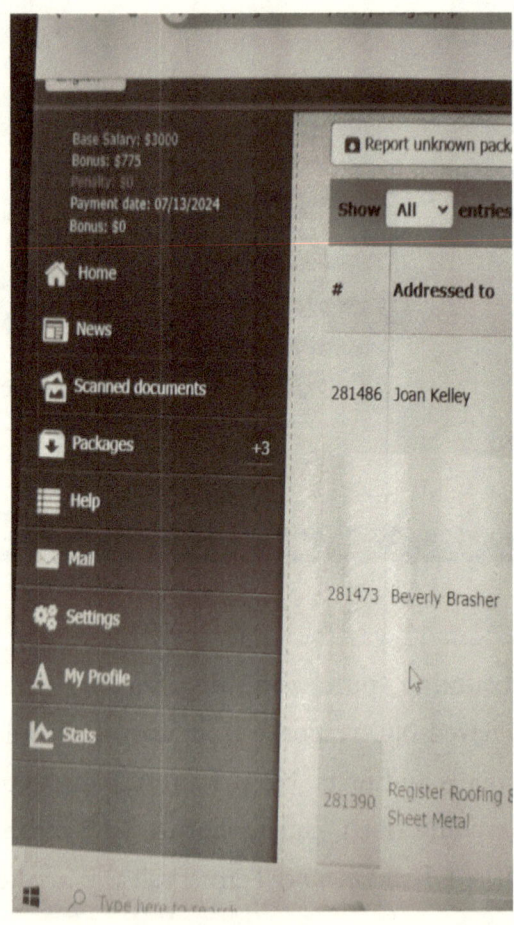

Update:

The apartment manager came to me and stated that she never had issues with me and I explained to her what had happened to me. She stated that she was sorry I went through this and she did not want me to have an eviction under my name. She was reaching out to corporate to do a stop eviction since it was one day and she would email me a broken lease so that I could apply for another apartment in the near future. As a result I had to go live with a family member.

I had the last item due to I never recieved a label to ship the item. Also, I was not paid and I kept it as evidence it was under $27.12. I have the dealership who ordered it from Jacksonville, Florida.

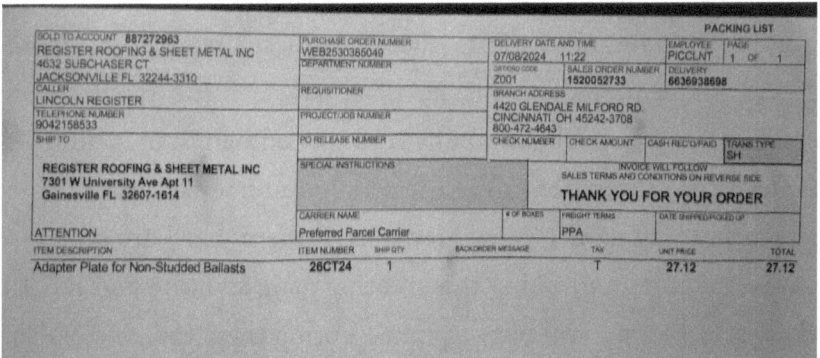

This is the package:

I have been unlawfully terminated, disability, abuse of power, wage theft, identity theft, discrimination, retaliation, labor & employment, federal / state labor law, whistle blower, and emotional distress. The company is a legit company, but is running under a false advertisement to use people and not pay them. I have researched ways and I know how to find them, but I am going to have legal help in presuing this to bring gang stalking and RICO charges to them. I will not stop until I bring them to justice! Also, if there is a lawyer who is reading this and wishes to reach out to me please contact me via email: winallyear23@gmail.com.

Also, I researched on Google that other individuals have been impacted by this company and hopefully by bringing awareness to the public these victims will recieve justice as well.

🔍 Find local businesses

# BBB Scam Tracker

‹ Back to search

❗ This content is based on victim and potential victim accounts. Government agencies and legitimate business names and phone numbers are often used by scam artists to take advantage of people.

Share and help us warn others

**Description**
It was a mule scam where packages would be shipped to my address, I'd print out the shipping labels. The company navigated through a dashboard on cshipping-dash.com and they were would call from different numbers with the same area code. I was never compensated.

**Targeted Person's Location**
IL, USA- 60411

**Scammer Information**
📍 Fall River, MA- 02720

✉ notifications@shipdepcargill.com

📱 (508) 217-9921

🌐 cshipping-dash.com

◀     ●     ▦

Cargill Shipping
Katey Shaw
HR Department

508-316-5955

888-688-2599

Frances Dixon

Manager

508-939-5615

Cloe Ross

508-351-0590

Rose Morris

508-217-9921

Accounting Team

888-688-2599

1 Ace St Unit 12, Fall River, MA 02720

# REGIONS BANK

Now, this is the one I feel like took me for a real turn of events due to the following: racial profiling, discrmination, abuse of power, defamation of character, pain and suffering. I believed banks were meant to make you feel safe and secure and my experience at Regions Bank was far from that experience. I intially deposited a check at my personal checking at Chase Bank and then I decided it would be released sooner if I went to another bank. Chase then endorsed the check and told me the bank will know that the check was not deposited into my account. I took the check to the bank and they told me it would be a 7 day hold on the check and I stated no problem on 6/04/2024.

When I went to the bank on 6/04/24 I deposited the check into the account. Upon checking my wallet the next day, I was missing my id and my bank card. I looked everywhere and realized the only place I had went was to the bank. I called the bank and the branch employee stated the teller made a honest mistake and did not put the identification card as well as bank card in the envelope. He only put the deposit slip and I didn't check it until I got home. (I am feeling as if I was targeted).The check was released and I went the bank to make a withdrawal I waited 15 minutes in the drive thru and was told to come inside because the amount was a large amount. So, I went inside and the teller had the money sitting on the counter. I gave the teller my id and bank card then I was told that a hold was placed on the money and it can't be released. I told him that's wierd so I went to the branch manager office to find out what's going on.

The branch manager name is Ange Banda in Gainesville and she was at first telling me a whole different story. She told me that the money did not clear and it was returned. She went to the printer to retrieve papers and tell me that is why I have a -$7.75 balance on the account. I told her that is not true, because it came out of my client who I was working for as a virtual assistant. I signed a NDA when I started working with him, because I plan his trips, search for venues, and gifts, etc...I explained to her that was not true and she would not simply stop LYING!. So, I was constantly back in forth to the bank placing tickets to correct this issue and the other teller she did not really know what to do so a male baranch came and assisted her with the ticket. Then, I kept calling from the bank to Operations and Fraud Department. So, now they are saying I have placed a fradulent check to them. There was another check by a different individual who wrote a check that was returned and Angie Banda states it was that check which was not true and misleading.

Check on hold:

Thanks for messaging R 7/15/24 Charlene! My name is Iris H. I'll be happy to assist you today.

There appears to be a branch level hold on the account. We can absolutely get you more information on this, but it would require that you visit the lobby of your local branch.
Most of our branches no longer require an appointment to step inside the lobby. However, if you would like to avoid any potential wait times, you may set an appointment online.
You can easily set up an appointment with your local branch online at regions.com by clicking the "Make an Appointment" link from the bottom of any page.
• Select Customer Type
• Select an appointment topic
• Select a branch location
• Select a date and time for the appointment
• Click the "Schedule It" button to submit the appointment

9:35 PM

I have visited the branch and the ticket completer last Friday

Sent 9:36 PM

I have visited the branch 5 times and 3 tickets

Sent 9:37 PM

I understand. It is a branch level hold which means Contact Center Bankers do not have access to the account and any and all questions regarding the account would have to be addressed at a branch. My apologies for the inconvenience.

Write a message                    SEND

Then, I was advised by the customer service to go to another bank. I traveled an hour away to Leesburg, Florida to complete a ticket stayed ther for an hour just to call a few days later that the customer service or that department stated they do not have one ticket. I was so upset I did lose my cool because I had been more than patient with them. One thing the branch gave me was a printed out form stated exactly what I told the branch manager in Gainesville, Florida. Online mobile banking displayed the available balance on 6/13/2024. Wait....Not only have the bank been holding my money, the money became available and monthly fee came out of the money that she state was denied. I was going to add another client but their initial payment did not clear and so I decided to not move forward with her. The branch manager tried to state the the check didn't clear for that potential client was actually for my current client.

The branch manager stated the money was not in the account it was available:

| Date | Type | Amount | Serial Number | Tran Code | Description | Cu |
|------|------|--------|---------------|-----------|-------------|-----|
| 06/28/2024 | Debit | $ 7.00 | | 0000 | MONTHLY FEE | |
| 06/04/2024 | Credit | $ 10,625.00 | | DEPOSIT | DEPOSIT | |
| 06/03/2024 | Debit | $ 1,850.10 | | 0051 | RETURNED DEPOSIT ITEM OF ITM | |
| 05/31/2024 | Debit | $ 7.00 | | 0000 | MONTHLY FEE | |
| 05/30/2024 | Credit | $ 1,850.10 | 9371158001 | 0185 | MOBILE DEPOSIT | |
| 05/09/2024 | Debit | $ 83.75 | 3001611248 | 0158 | ATM WITHDRAWAL | |
| 05/09/2024 | Debit | $ 3.00 | 3002028442 | 0047 | ATM FEE | |
| 04/30/2024 | Debit | $ 7.00 | | 0000 | MONTHLY FEE | |

ARCHER RD
07/16/2024 02:49PM
Account: XXXXXXX3109
* Projected Available Balance is the anticipated available balance after the next nightly posting. Deposits made reflected in the projected available balance but may not be available to cover transactions until the following posting.

I went back to the Regions bank in Gainesville, because you are not only holding my money, but you have not callled or emailed so I can understand WHY you are holding the money. I spoke with Domique a branch assistant at the bank who gave me a printout stating the check had been suspected of fraud, because someone stated the check had already been cashed. How in the world is that possible? I told her I initially went to my personal checking then came there, because I thought it would clear sooner. She said no one really understood what was going on so she now it makes perfect sense with the endorsement from the bank. I told her there was no communication on there end to reach out to me or even verify it from Chase. She explained to me that he bank does not verify with another bank. She made another ticket to electronic banking and software. It has been another week and I am still getting no results. I told her that I have facing eviction and I was working three jobs and not able to pay rent. I have never experienced this type of nightmare in my life!

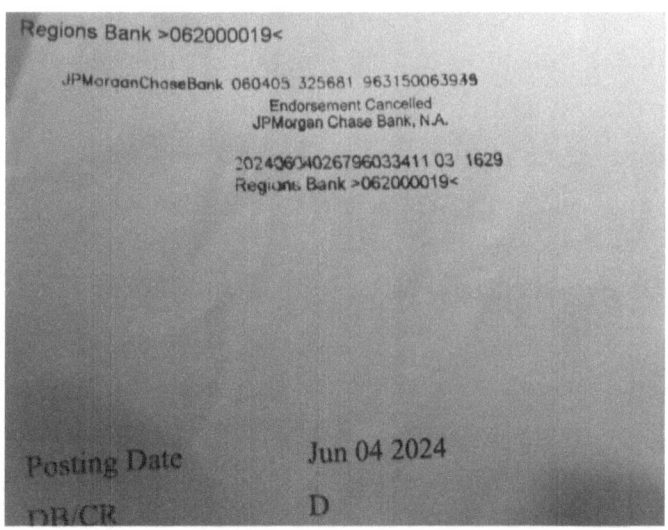

Then, I waited a few days to call and speak with the branch manager in Gainesville, Fl. Her story had changed and she was now saying the money is in the bank. She will create another ticket while I'm on the phone and she don't understand why they are just holding the money. I am just sitting her and running back and forth to the bank until it is resolved. Right! Wrong, I am going through an injustice and I am about to lawyer up, because I feel I have a few lawsuits on my hand!

This occurred the 2nd week of July:

When I contact the bank one day the branch manager stated hi my friend how are you doing. Which threw me completely off, because I would not consider her a friend.

Now, I'm feeling lost, imagine doing everything right and it still went wrong. It takes a special kind of hate to harm someone who has never did anything to you. My anxiety was through the roof of getting the knock on the door and having to leave within a certain timeframe. I worked so much I just would simply crash out and finding time to write my book. I had to have alot of self - talks and listen to motivational speakers, because what was after me was strong, but their errors were greater.

It's Friday 7/19/2024 and I called the Regions bank and Dominque stated the ticket she made was to understand why the hold was placed on my account. I told her I thought the ticket was to release the hold off of the account. She stated that the only person who can send for a hold to be released is the Branch manager. WOW!

Dominique stated the check was registered to my name and not the business name.

If you have a business bank account with your account with your company's name and your name as the owner or authorized agent, you can usually cash the check at a local branch by endorsing it and verifying your identity (experian.com/blogs). In case your bank doesn't allow you to cash the check for some reason, you can simply deposit into your account- just about anyone can deposit a business check into the company's business checking account (experian.com/blogs).

I told her the check has cleared over a month ago that is irrelevant. She said it's possible they may return the money. How can you return money that I have already worked for unbelievable? Dominique asked me to reach out to the client to the client to issue another check so it can go through quicker. The money has ALREADY CLEARED! So, I reached out to my client and he honestly thought I was trying to scam him after I told him my conversation with the branch assistant. As, a result I lost my client. I went into the branch with the mindset to sit back and allow her to talk and maybe something will slip out on 7/22/2024. I asked her where I am at in the process for the hold to be released. She stated it was sent for investigation to Operations and Fraud Department to Regions Check & Deposit Fraud Monitoring Department. She stated no motion to close account and no changes on the account. The account was negative and the check made it positive and now on the 7/28/2024 will be the 2nd time the monthly fees come out of the money they have on hold.

Once a check has cleared, it cannot be reversed unless fraud or identity theft is suspected (Google.com). If that was the case the check had cleared available in my account for over a period of time. What is baffling to me is that the bank would not allow me to take money out of the bank yet they took out monthly fees.

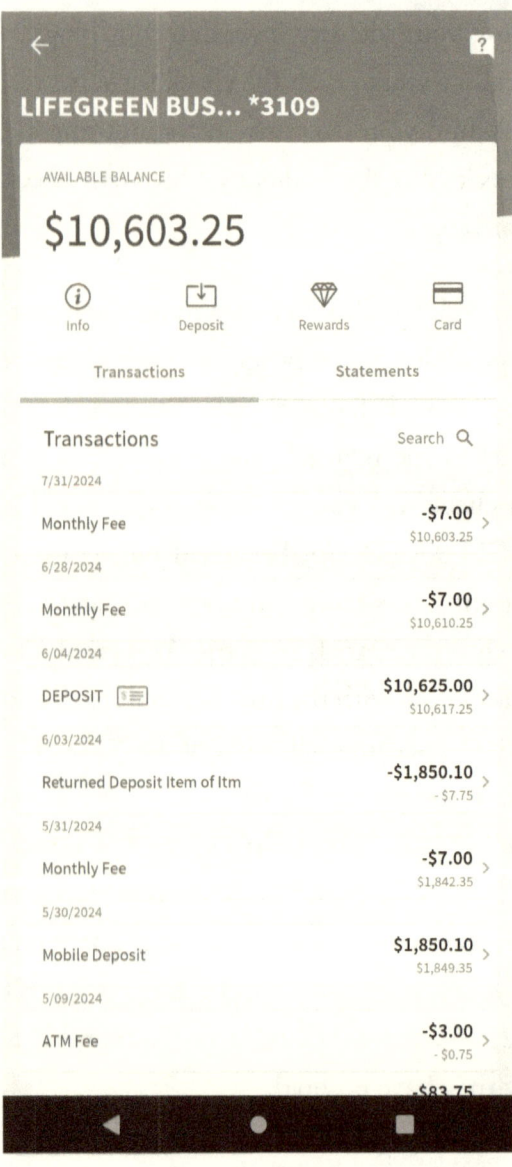

I asked her to request a release of funds and she stated that she can't do that because of the department. I told Ange Banda the three tickets at the Gainesville branch and the Regions branch in The Villages, Florida did not show up on the customer service department. Ange told me that the branch manager no longer has his position in the The Villages, Florida, but little do she know I was sent a survey on her call and I left very detailed information about my interactions with her. She disregarded me losing so much and just told me to wait until the investigation is complete. WOW! I am constantly checking emails, phone calls and the mobile app daily while seeking a consultation.

Consumer Laws in Florida set out to protect residents from scams and enforce their rights against both the government and large corporations (Google.com).

I had exhausted all my ideas, traveling to the bank and calling the bank. I had called the 1-800 number for regions and the department who was handling it. The woman made a statement and laughed if they give the money to me. I asked her what do you mean if you give me my money. I knew at that moment I needed outside help and I started emailing lawyers. I received responses, but one particular lawyer was very empathetic on 7/24/24. Although, she will like to iniate a consultation with the firm, she will like me to file a complaint with the Federal Reserve Board which is Regions Bank Primary Regulator to try to resolve it without paying a fee due to I already lost alot.

The initial process click on the link and complete the steps.

https://forms.federalreserveconsumerhelp.gov/secure/complaint/complaintType.html

The steps to complete is the following: your personal info, routing #, Bank address, phone number, and have a brief description to copy and paste or type. Each time you leave the website you have to start over, but the process is not long.

No supporting documents will be accepted at that time.

When I looked on Google I like to conduct my research and try to find if there are individuals who experienced what I have experienced before. Below you will view a customer of Regions Bank and an attorney that answered his question.

Banks implement check holds to protect themselves and their customers from potential financial losses. Here are the key reasons why banks might hold your check:

Reasons for Check Holds

Check Verification: Banks need to ensure the check is legitimate and that the issuing bank has sufficient funds to cover the amount

New Accounts: Banks may place holds on checks deposited by new customers to assess their financial history and prevent potential fraud

Redeposits: If a check was previously returned for insufficient funds, the bank may hold it again to avoid further losses

Large Deposits: Checks exceeding a certain amount, typically $5,525, might be held to verify the funds and prevent potential overdrafts

Banking History: If your account has a history of overdrafts or suspicious activity, the bank may hold checks to mitigate risk

Suspected Fraud: If the bank suspects the check is fraudulent, it will hold it for investigation before releasing the funds

Emergency Situations: In cases of natural disasters or other emergencies that disrupt banking operations, the bank may hold checks until normal operations resume (Google.com).

Duration of Check Holds

The duration of a check hold varies depending on the circumstances and the bank's policies (Google.com). However, federal regulations limit the maximum hold period. Generally, most checks should be cleared within two business days (Google.com). However, exceptions exist for larger checks, new accounts, or when the bank has reasonable cause to doubt the check's validity (Google.com). In such cases, the hold can extend up to seven business days (Google.com).

I researched through Google and found out someone had a similar experience as mine a few years ago Below is his question to the attorney and and the attorney's response.

## How long can regions hold a freeze on my checking account due to investigating a mobile deposit that the funds are cleared on?

I had a payroll deposit come into my account in the early days of Oct. 2019, the deposit was placed on hold for several days, then released then placed on hold a second time for a matter of 13 days then again made to be an available balance at which then regions bank put a freeze on my account and said they were investigating the transaction to protect against fraud. This was in October, I have been fighting back and forth with them for months now and gotten verification from the depositing company, the paying bank, and the check has cleared and the funds never bounced back and even the paying company has verified the my bank that the funds are indeed legit and for sure did come from and were paid from their account as well and that their payee was infact myself. its now been 7 entire lonnnng months, I need some advice please

Asked in Hudson, FL | Apr 10, 2020 | 1 answer

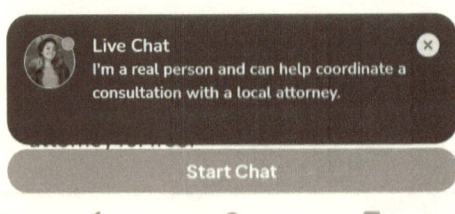

**Live Chat** ✕
I'm a real person and can help coordinate a consultation with a local attorney.

**Start Chat**

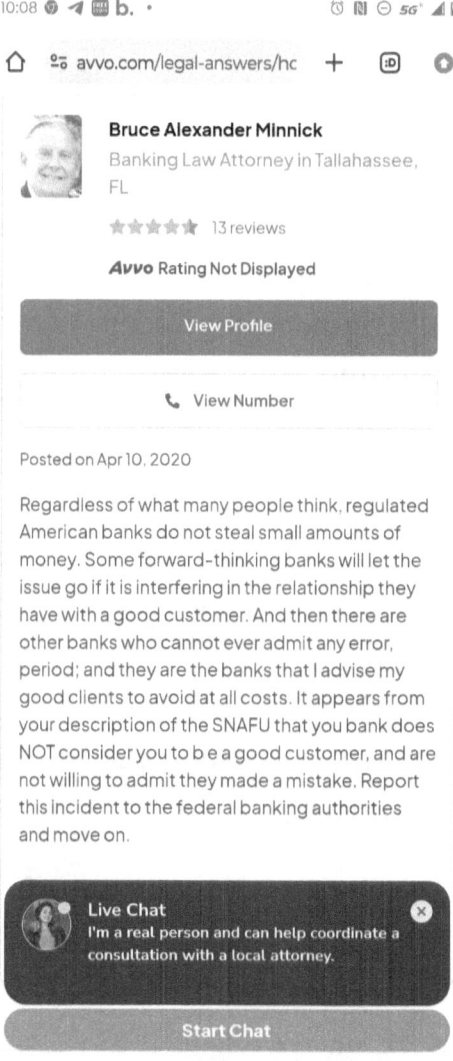

**Bruce Alexander Minnick**

Banking Law Attorney in Tallahassee, FL

★ ★ ★ ★ ★   13 reviews

***Avvo*** Rating Not Displayed

| View Profile |
| :---: |

📞   View Number

Posted on Apr 10, 2020

Regardless of what many people think, regulated American banks do not steal small amounts of money. Some forward-thinking banks will let the issue go if it is interfering in the relationship they have with a good customer. And then there are other banks who cannot ever admit any error, period; and they are the banks that I advise my good clients to avoid at all costs. It appears from your description of the SNAFU that you bank does NOT consider you to b e a good customer, and are not willing to admit they made a mistake. Report this incident to the federal banking authorities and move on.

**Live Chat**  ✕
I'm a real person and can help coordinate a consultation with a local attorney.

| Start Chat |
| :---: |

◀        ●        ■

At this present time I have moved almost 3 hours away and I went to another Regions Bank. I spoke with a branch manager Brodrick Wells Sr. and gave him a narrative of what has occurred. I went into the bank to ask for a hold to be placed for removal.

The branch manager stated that he could get fired if he document on 8/01/24 in a different city. He stated there is way too many people involved and someone else who works at the bank stated it's too messy after she reviewed the notes and immediately left the office. He stated that the account hold had been released from reading his notes, the account was set for closure and the available money in the account would be released by September the 9th. I went to The Villages Florida the branch manager stated my complaint previously (while I was living in Gainesville, Florida), placed a request to corporate and other information he was fired and the branch manager of Gainesville told me he is no longer with the company. On August 2nd Janette from the Regions Response team for the survey I completed called me and they filed a complaint against the branch manager in Gainesville, Florida today. The Federal Reserve is now investigating Regions Bank in Gainesville, Florida and corporate.

When I start to think about why am I waiting for money that is off hold and I should be able to make a withdrawal from. I called the villages to speak with a branch manager and a branch manager acting in for one day stated he would place a hold to be removed and call back. I never recieved a callback. I called the next day and he went to another branch. I spoke with someone else there that stated there was no hold on the money. It's available and I can come make a withdrawal. I went to the tailor requesting a withdrawal on 8/07/24 he stated the amount was large asked me to come in. Then he came to me stating I had to speak with the branch manager for an apparant hold on the money and he had worked an half day.

Now I am like this is more than insane what in the world is going on and everyone is lying at this point covering up to protect from a lawsuit. I called the branch to speak to Brodrick and he changed his story saying he did not say that and the bank fraud department does not want to give the money to me. I had a witness who sat in there with me and heard hime say something totally different.

When I spoke with the villages where I opened it up it stated that it was still be verified not knowing that I knew the hold was off. So she had asked me where I went I wouldn't say. She said she will call me back regarding the hold and if I can go to the bank to get the money. Unfortunately, that individual did not call me back either. It's unfortunate that I had to go through this for a senseless deceptive cover up and misrepresentation of information. Whatever is in those notes are very incriminating and it's a big cover up! I am waiting for the Federal Reserve to go through those notes.

Regions Bank
3710 SW 38th Street Gainesville, Fl. 32608
352-244-8250

# CONCLUSION

Shopify my experiences occured over the years of repeatedly knowing something was wrong, but I couldn't prove it. These other issues I faced happened in 2024 and it has damaged me to the point were I was stripped of everything I had and yet I fought so back so I would not become broken. This all happened to me repeatedly with no chance to come up for air, and I know that it was only God who kept me from losing my mind! I bring awareness with names, locations, and numbers so that it can help others to not go through what I went through. I will start a blog to inform others and keep the website up and running by continuing to expose companies who think they can get away with harming innocent people.

I look forward in the upcoming book with my life story in which was more detrimental and traumatic experiences that some people would have lived two lives to occur. There will be a TV appearance so that I can go on there to update the details and tell my side of the story as well reach so many people to bring down corrupted companies who take damaging the lives of others to an all time high. I thank you for purchasing my eBook and allowing me to share my experiences with you!

I will be looking forward to share my next eBook with you titled, "They Tried To Kill Me To Keep Their Secrets"!

www.ingramcontent.com/pod-product-compliance
Lightning Source LLC
Chambersburg PA
CBHW031228120626
46545CB00003B/1030